HERE'S A HERO: DANIEL

TAMING THE LIONS IN YOUR LIFE

HERE'S A HERO: DANIEL

Taming the Lions in Your Life

Les Morgan

CHRISTIAN PUBLICATIONS
CAMP HILL, PENNSYLVANIA

To Les Jr. and Philip,
my two sons who think I am a hero,
and I hope to never disappoint.
May God shape you both to be heroes

Christian Publications
3825 Hartzdale Drive, Camp Hill, PA 17011

The mark of ✝ *vibrant faith*

ISBN: 0-87509-479-1
LOC Catalog Card Number: 91-58677
© 1992 by Christian Publications
All rights reserved
Printed in the United States of America

92 93 94 95 96   5 4 3 2 1

Cover photo courtesy of John Edwards, Denver Zoo
Cover design by Step One Design

Contents

Foreword

━━━━━━━━

There is an interesting bit of trivia about the U.S. Air Force Academy that tells us a lot about the society we live in today. The Academy has very strict admission requirements, yet they have found they must accept 400 more applicants than they need every year. The reason is the strict honor code of the Academy; a cadet caught in the smallest of lies will be immediately drummed out.

We're living in an age where integrity is in very short supply. Every day we confront temptations, pressures and problems that, like a pack of hungry lions, are threatening to eat us alive. It's not surprising that, according to Josh McDowell, "young people today . . . are crying out for role models of men and women who have it together in love, marriage, sex and family."

I thank God for heroes in the Bible like Daniel, who show us the way to tame the lions in our lives.

And I thank God for heroes of today like Les Morgan. Les makes Daniel come alive on these pages, and shows how this Hebrew teenager fought and won the same battles that confront teens today. Les has been in the battle himself, so he knows what he's talking about, and he knows how to win. That's why I call him a hero. That's why I call him my friend.

"God is preparing his heroes," A.B. Simpson declared, "and when the opportunity comes He can fit them into their place in a moment and the world will wonder where they came from." Are you ready to meet this challenge? Then read this book, apply its principles, and become a lion-tamer, like Daniel. Or like Les Morgan.

Dan Bergstrom
Director of Youth
The Christian and Missionary Alliance

Preface

Whenever God wants to do something big, He often taps a teenager on the shoulder and says, "How about you?"

This can be seen in many lives throughout Scripture: Joseph, Josiah, Jeremiah, Mark, Timothy, Esther, and Mary, the mother of Jesus, for example. Current history follows that same pattern: Billy Graham, Josh McDowell, Chuck Swindoll, Tony Campolo, and Joni Erickson Tada.

I believe God is raising up genuine champions and heroes that will set this world on its ear. Godly, Spirit-filled teenagers are getting a call from heaven to be different. And to the shock of many, they are responding and daring to take the risks involved.

That is why role models and heroes from the Bible like Daniel are important. Daniel puts the reality of hardships, abuse, threats, slavery, countries at war, social injustice, lies and deception into the context of living a godly life—despite those things being hurled at a person all at once. His life challenges us to come out of the grandstand, get onto the field and make a difference. Any wimp can "go with the flow"; Daniel issues a dare to be a warrior, a winner and a hero.

When all is said and done, being a hero God's way is the only thing worthwhile. The Hero of heroes, Jesus, will reward those who took the challenge and made a difference.

I am grateful to many who played important roles as I wrote. Laura Stikeleather, Christine Henry and Jeanna Sutera, along with maintaining academic loads at college, also served as my secretaries. I am grateful to each for their contribution and assistance. I am also thankful to Jon Graf and Dave Fessenden of Christian Publications for their encouragement. I believe this project has been enhanced by their friendship and skills.

Also, as in every other book I have written before, I am grateful to my wife, Kay. Her support was demonstrated best when, after I told her I was finally through, she gave me a big hug and said, "Thank you for your hard work, honey. I know you will make a difference in some people's lives."

I am also indebted to Campus Community Church and Toccoa Falls College for their support. It is my great honor to be the Campus Pastor where God is raising up many warriors and champions and is forming heroes from scratch.

The affirmation of having Dan Bergstrom, National Youth Director of The Christian and Missionary Alliance, write the Foreword is also something for which I express thanks. His shared vision of seeing teenagers impact our world and make a difference in Jesus' name links us together.

Most of all, I thank the Hero of Heroes, Jesus, for giving me an opportunity to know the change that He brings to a life. He, as well, has honored me by allowing me to plant seed in the lives of others that they too may know this change and take it to yet others.

A long time ago, God raised up a hero from a teenager named Daniel. The world has stood dumb-founded since then whenever his story has been told. May God repeat that process again. In a day when our world needs a change-agent, a risk-taker and a hero who will point them to the One who will one day settle all wrongs and end all conflicts, may God issue a challenge to a future hero that will astonish an evil-bent world.

Les Morgan
Toccoa Falls College

1

Winners vs. Wimps

Tina **Turner sings,** "We Don't Need Another Hero," but she couldn't be more wrong. We don't need another wimp, but we do need heroes—those who are winners, who have the guts to take some risks.

We all need a hero to admire. In fact, I have never met anyone who didn't have a hero. Some heroes stand for good, others for evil. But one thing is for sure. Everyone has a hero. Even heroes have heroes.

Heroes give inspiration and stir ambition. They give us courage to excel even at our lowest point. They make us want to win whether we play sports or play music, run cross-country or across campus, watch the news or make the news. Heroes issue challenges. Without challenges, we would yawn our way through life. And who wants to do that?

Tony Campolo surely didn't—he wanted a challenge! It all started when, as a teenager growing up in West Philadelphia, a friend named "Mush" questioned Campolo's bravery.

Campolo and his friends used to play a game called stickball, which involved using the handles from brooms to bat a ball around the neighborhood. Usually the noise would become so loud the police would be called and confiscate all the sticks, thus ending the game.

One day while sitting on a curb wishing they had something to do, Campolo said, "Somebody ought to get into the back room of that police station where the cops store all those sticks they take from us and steal some of them back." It was here that Campolo heard these sinister words from "Mush": "I dare you!"

Campolo tells what happened next:

When Mush said that, I reacted like a Pavlovian dog. Like a lot of boys, I had been conditioned to react to dares in ways that are hard to describe. My back would tighten. My blood would run hot. My heart would beat faster. All of this happened in response to the simple words, "I dare you."

"All right," I snapped. "You guys go into the police station before me, talk to those cops, and keep them occupied. Pretend that you have to do a term paper for school about police work. While you've got their attention, I'll get into that back room and I'll come out with five sticks or I

7

won't come out at all!"

I want you to know that the name Tony Campolo is still legend in West Philadelphia. The kids on the street still talk about the guy who robbed the police station at 55th and Pine.

Some kids get a thrill out of going to Disneyland. Others get a thrill out of riding the roller coaster at the Magic Mountain amusement park. Some get turned on by surfing. But if you climb the highest mountain or zip the tracks of the world's fastest roller coaster, you still won't know the exhilaration that comes from robbing a police station. I was on a high for three months! I was so pumped up with adrenalin that I bounced around for days like a jack ball.[1]

Tony Campolo—what a wild man! It's no wonder he challenges teens to be heroes—it was imbedded in him as a teen in West Philly! He was brave enough to do something stupid like take broomsticks from a police station, yet he later turned that boldness into something positive for God!

Jennifer Capriati is a hero. At 13 years, 11 months old, she took a risk that most people wouldn't even dream about: she became the youngest professional tennis player in history. At 14, Jennifer played in the French Open, competing against veteran players. What an example of courage and bravery she is! She has the stuff to be a hero. It didn't come without risks, without a price to pay. But being a hero never does. It means you make a decision to respond with all your might to the challenges and become determined to win, even when the quitters fade off the scene.

Winners vs. Wimps

Not all heroes are so winsome; some are wimps. A few years ago, Len Bias was the talk of pro basketball. Then we found out the truth:

It's June 17, 1986. The place is New York City's Felt Forum. It is the first round of the National Basketball Association draft, and Len Bias is the happiest guy in the world. Commissioner David Stern has just called Bias's name over the loud speaker. Someone hands him a green Celtics hat, and his 6 foot 8 inch, well-muscled body moves toward the podium.

For two years he has been ACC player of the year with an average of 20.9 points a game. He finished as Maryland's all-time leading scorer with 2,149 points. Even rival North Carolina State coach Jim Valvano said, "Lenny was almost the perfect basketball player: the body, the quickness, the jumping ability." In his four years at Maryland, he never missed a game due to injury.

This moment he stands in front of dozens of microphones and a screaming crowd with what seems to be nothing but success stretching out in front of him like an endless expressway. Reebok shoe company has agreed to a Bias endorsement that would provide him with financial security for life. Larry Bird is so ecstatic that he even promises to show up at rookie camp since Bias will be there.

There is just one problem: forty hours from now, 22-year-old Lenny Bias will be dead of cardiorespiratory arrest. The state medical examiner will quickly determine that cocaine killed him. The redness in his windpipe and the congestion in his mucous membrane will help determine that Bias freebased cocaine. A high concentration of the drug will be found in his blood—6.5 milligrams per liter. His successful future will have disappeared in a vapor.

Even though he wasn't pushy about his conviction, his friends and family called Bias a card-carrying, born-again Christian. He had a reputation around his teammates for being a straight kid, a non-drug user. But something went terribly wrong. Late that Wednesday night Bias compromised his convictions and decided to forget his reputation. Somehow, his values were turned upside down. What he said he would never do was now history. The unthinkable had happened. He got stoned. His heart stopped ticking. His friends panicked. They called emergency, but the rescue unit was too late. His life was wasted. Drugs buried another victim. What might have been went down the drain.[2]

Unless heroes are heroes God's way, they become wimps. What baseball fan wasn't disappointed when

Pete Rose was sentenced to jail for illegal gambling while playing for the Cincinnati Reds? Who isn't disturbed when political leaders come tumbling down nose-first for cheating, lying, and fakery? When famous preachers and evangelists get caught in adultery?

And when the news broke that some Marines had exchanged secret information for what they thought would be secret sex with Russian women, it made Americans' blood boil. It's enough to make a person want to stand up and shout:

"WHERE ARE THE HEROES? HAVE THEY ALL BECOME WIMPS?"

Look at Jimi Hendrix. Proclaimed the hero of guitar players, he overdosed on drugs and drowned in his own vomit.

The "King," Elvis Presley, was "crowned" the leading entertainer of all history, but something went wrong. No one danced as the news spread—Elvis was found on his bathroom floor, curled up in the fetal position, dead. The body of this one-time hero couldn't handle the drugs injected into it.

Marilyn Monroe, the beauty queen of the screen, was found dead in her apartment, apparently by suicide. The same is true of John Belushi of Saturday Night Live, and Dennis Wilson of the Beach Boys. Though all were role models and heroes, in the end they "wimped out."

Their lifestyles proved they weren't winners. Anybody can drink booze, bake their brain with drugs, sleep around and be a fake. It takes someone with courage and guts to be different.

11

That is why teens today are asking questions like these:

"Is anybody for real?"
"Can I really trust anybody?"
"Is there a person left on this planet who is genuine?"
"Where are the heroes? Do I have any options besides the rockers, the surfers, and the dopers to live my life by?"

Recently, I heard Dawson McAlister speak at a conference on the teenagers of today. As he reeled off the following statistics, I was more convinced than ever that we need heroes who have more to offer than a good time, a "buzz" and a one-way ride to the cemetery:

- 70 percent of today's teens do not go to church
- 50 percent live in one parent families
- 1,500,000 run away from home every year
- 250,000 teenage girls are prostitutes
- 50,000 run away every year and are never heard from again by their parents
- 5,000 are buried with no identity
- 5,000,000 have drinking problems
- 3,000 a day get pregnant, with half of those pregnancies ending at an abortion clinic.[3]

Don't Be Ripped Off

It's hard to know what hero to follow. No one wants to get ripped off. It's even harder being a hero. Taking that challenge costs commitment, consistency, and courage. Those things can't be picked up at a "blue light special" at K-Mart! Those characteristics require daring to be different, and viewing life distinctively. That is so rare, some people have given up on heroes today. As one teen said, "Being a total hero isn't possible today."[4]

It's true—you can't be a wimp, and be a winner too. The two are not a match. It's like skiing and reading a book at the same time; it just doesn't work. The reason is a wimp doesn't deserve an audience, but a hero is worth listening to.

How can you tell the difference? Any "Joe Blow" can claim to be hero, but do they deserve your attention? For starters, a standard is needed.

Standards for Hero Candidates

Here are some questions that may start us thinking about what a hero is.

1. Is this person honest? Genuine? For real?
2. Do they have "the stuff"? Are they seeking after the status of a hero, or do they really have something to offer?
3. What will happen if I follow their lifestyle? Will I be ripped off, kicked in the teeth, or end up in a morgue? Or will there be a contribution made to me, others and the world?
4. What are they like when no one is looking? Are they the same as when everyone is patting them on the back, telling them how great they are?
5. Would God approve of them? Are they worth my

life (my *only* life) being spent by living like them?
6. Do they take risks that are worth taking, or are they on an ego trip that satisfies their need to be in the forefront?

These questions are serious. So is trusting your life to someone.

It's tough when you are lied to, rejected and left. It's like being violated when we trust someone only to have them take the best of what we have to offer and leave. When that happens, it's enough to make us wretch!

That's why we need winners and heroes, not wimps. Real heroes will contribute to us, not rob us. A genuine hero will be real even if no one is watching. They will be the same when all eyes are on them. They think of others, not just themselves. They are willing to pay the price of being a hero, which means being consistent and honest even in hard times.

If ever there was a guy who knew about hard times, it was Daniel. He knew heartache, abuse, rejection—yet through it all, he stayed true to God's ways. As a role model, he shines like a light in a dark cave. Daniel is a hero, a winner who deserves our attention. When we choose to live life like Daniel, we *will* win !

A Warrior Who Isn't a Wimp

Daniel's life is amazing. As a teen between the ages of 13 and 15 he endured:

- being taken from his family, never to see them again.
- seeing his nation destroyed by another country.
- becoming a slave in a strange land.
- having to cope with a new language, new customs and strange food.
- being given a different name, changing his identity as a person.
- a "deprogramming" where everything he had been told about God, living and how to be a real person was laughed at, made fun of, and ridiculed.
- going to a special school for approximately three years where he was told how he was to act, think, be, talk, eat, study, and conduct himself—with no options.
- being lied about, set up for a trap, and hated for being honest.

In spite of incredible pressure, Daniel fought through these wars and surfaced a hero. Daniel consistently honored the Lord's ways. Though he was put into a lion's den for loving God, he didn't compromise. Daniel wasn't a wimp–he was a warrior for God. His courage is worth modeling. And his relationship with the Lord is one that impresses even the most skeptical person anywhere.

As you study Daniel, refer back to the standards for a hero and see how Daniel matches up. Here's a promise: you won't be disappointed. In reading and studying this hero, ask the Lord for the strength Daniel found. You will find our God wants to do just that, for He loves to see others become heroes.

Do you need courage? Strength? Power? Do you wonder if the Lord can make you a winner and a warrior? Just watch as the life of Daniel, a normal teenager, unfolds and blossoms into a real hero. Then allow his life to be reproduced in you. While the price to pay isn't cheap, there will never be any regrets for letting God do in you what he did in a teen named Daniel long ago.

We need heroes. Can God create one in you?

Putting It into My Life

1. Why do heroes inspire and give courage? What makes them different? What people do you consider heroes? Why?

2. How do heroes become wimps? Why is it so disappointing? Have you been disappointed like that? When?

3. If you had a chance to talk to Jimi Hendrix, Elvis Presley, Marilyn Monroe or others like them, what would you say to them? What would be your questions? How do you think they would respond?

4. Do you know someone who is being lied to by a person they consider a hero? How do you think they feel? What would you like to say to them? Could you talk to them today?

2

The Toughest Test Ever

Tests are a part of life. Most teens look forward to tests like they look forward to a toothache. Mention the word "exam" to the average teenager, and he or she will break out into a cold sweat and turn a light shade of green. One teen got so nervous when the teacher announced a test, he got a pass to the restroom and hasn't been seen since.

There is one test, however, that most teens enjoy. It comes when a person turns 16. It's called the driving test.

I remember my 16th birthday. I came out of bed like I was fired out of a cannon, got dressed, and inhaled breakfast on my way out the door. Although the Florida Highway Patrol office didn't open until 8:00 a.m., I was sitting on the front steps by 7:30. I couldn't wait to take *that* test! I was ready for any question fired my way. I had *devoured* that driver's manual. In fact, in looking back on that time, had I studied in school as hard as I did for that driving test, I could have been a brain surgeon!

A test can be a pop quiz, fill-in-the-blank, unit exam, essay or oral exam. My favorite one was "multiple guess"—you know—cover your eyes and fill in whatever little square on the answer sheet your pencil lands on.

There are also physical tests. Drill sergeants love to give these to new recruits. So do football coaches. Every August, all across America, coaches with whistles clenched between their teeth have people running through tires, jumping over each other, throwing somebody to the ground, catching balls, tackling, tumbling, grunting and growling until they see dots. Basketball players can relate. They are assigned to a coach who has one mission in life—to see how long it takes for a team to wear out the protective coating on the wooden floor by having them run up and down the court. Swimmers can identify, also. Their coaches test them by clocking the amount of time it takes a team to drink the entire contents of a pool while swimming 5,000 laps—without coming up for air. The same is true for tennis players. They are tested by their coaches by counting the number of times it takes to knock all the fuzz off a new tennis ball in 110-degree weather.

There are also pregnancy tests, Breathalyzer tests, blood tests and urine tests for drug use. And have you ever noticed that no one has to announce who scored the highest on the I.Q. tests? The class brain always blows that one away.

Tests can be frightening and stressful, yet they are important. They are frightening because of the fear of failure, and stressful because of the possibility of a poor performance. They also are important because they help set goals and show where we can improve and make positive changes. They show what we are doing right and how we can do better.

Another Kind of Test

Sometimes the Lord tests us. No cheating is allowed. Although no grade is put on the bulletin board, no team listing announced, and no jersey handed out, only winners are on this team. No wimp can pass this test—they don't have "the stuff." To be on this team requires faithfulness, determination and courage. Daniel and his three friends had the "stuff." Check it out:

> In the third year of the reign of Jehoiakim king of Judah, Nebuchadnezzar king of Babylon came to Jerusalem and besieged it. And the Lord delivered Jehoiakim king of Judah into his hand, along with some of the articles from the temple of God. These he carried off to the temple of his god in Babylonia and put in the treasure house of his god.
>
> Then the king ordered Ashpenaz, chief of his court officials, to bring in some of the Israelites from the royal family and the nobility—young men without any physical defect, handsome,

showing aptitude for every kind of learning, well informed, quick to understand, and qualified to serve in the king's palace. He was to teach them the language and literature of the Babylonians. (Daniel 1:1–4)

Throughout history, countries have invaded other territories, taking people captive. Families who undergo this horrible act of being uprooted are often separated for a lifetime. What stays in their minds are the scenes of children crying and screaming as soldiers stormed into a house taking captive their parents and other adults. Many people today are hurting from that occurring in Vietnam. They are not even sure if their family members are still alive.

When Daniel and his three friends were teens, Jerusalem was invaded by the armies of Babylon. These four teenagers were taken captive. They were chosen by a commander named Ashpenaz to be trained as servants of the wicked King Nebuchadnezzar. If ever there was a tough test given, it was when these young men were uprooted from all they had ever known and made slaves.

They understood the demands of being tested not only scholastically and physically, but emotionally and spiritually as well. All four were given exams, and all four received the same grade: "C" for courage.

Content of the Test

This test had several "entrance exams." Look what the Scripture tells us:

1. Young Men (Daniel 1:4a). This refers to their age. In the original language, it most likely means that Daniel and his friends were between the ages of thirteen and fifteen. Most teens that age are hanging out at the mall, trying to impress the opposite sex, or saving money to buy the latest computer game or CD. Not Daniel and his friends. They were beaten and forced into submission, and were told who was in charge—Babylon!

2. Without Any Physical Defect (1:4a). There was no indication of physical or mental difficulties. They were strong, well-defined physically, and carried themselves with confidence. No wimps were in that crowd.

3. Handsome (1:4a). Not only were they teen-agers, full of energy and physically fit, they were also good-looking. Tom Cruise and Kirk Cameron would not have anything on these guys.

4. Intelligent (1:4b). Notice the qualifications: "showing aptitude for every kind of learning, well informed, quick to understand" (1:4b). These guys not only were young, handsome and physically in top shape, but they also had brains! Everything from a new language, customs, history, dress, food, ways of greeting, gestures, tones of speech, and ways of doing things would be different. They had to learn these cultural differences quickly.

What an incredible demand, for going into a new culture always means making mistakes. Recently, I heard about a missionary who preached his first sermon shortly after arriving in Taiwan. Without realizing it, throughout his entire sermon he claimed Jesus Christ was a "little green frog" who had come to save the world from sin! Imagine the remarkable pressure that these teenagers were under in their new culture!

5. Qualified to Serve in the King's Palace (1:4b). Like the secret service agents who guard the President or personnel who work in Buckingham Palace with the royalty of England, so Daniel and his friends had to meet standards. They did it well.

> At the end of the time set by the king to bring them in, the chief official presented them to Nebuchadnezzar. The king talked with them, and he found none equal to Daniel, Hananiah, Mishael and Azariah; so they entered the king's service. In every matter of wisdom and under-standing about which the king questioned them, he found them ten times better than all the magicians and enchanters in his whole kingdom. (1:18–20)

In a rigorous attempt to reprogram their thinking and convictions, these teens were confronted daily with the Babylonian lifestyle. The cultural practices of satanic magic, astrology, false religion, and evil medicine were demonstrated in an attempt to show who was more powerful—Jehovah-God, or the gods of Babylon. Their heritage, value system, faith, and obedience were challenged, over-shadowed, and all but removed. They were stretched to the maximum. Even their names were changed:

Original Name	New Name & Meaning
Daniel	Belteshazzar, "lady of our king"
Hananiah	Shadrach, "the command of Abu"
Mishael	Meshach, "who is what God is"
Azariah	Abednego, "servant of the shining one"

What an exam! Some historians think that this went on for over three years! Yet in every area these teen slaves excelled. What backbone!

Today teens are still being confronted by satanic forces, black magic arts, false religions and evil practices. There are more pornography outlets than McDonald's in America. The exalting of the New Age movement is as popular as the latest dance by M.C. Hammer. Often rock stars promote satanic worship at their concerts. Tragically, that which honors God is being yanked down, tramped on, ridiculed and hauled through the mud. Yet despite this blatant attempt to destroy, God still has teens who are keeping their stand. Daniel and his friends refused to go any other way but the Lord's way. It took guts to stick with their convictions, but that is what is required to pass the test of courage. Notice their strength and boldness:

> But Daniel resolved not to defile himself with the royal food and wine, and he asked the chief official for permission not to defile himself this way. Now God had caused the official to show

favor and sympathy to Daniel, but the official told Daniel, "I am afraid of my lord the king, who has assigned your food and drink. Why should he see you looking worse than the other young men your age? The king would then have my head because of you."

Daniel then said to the guard whom the chief official had appointed over Daniel, Hananiah, Mishael and Azariah, "Please test your servants for ten days: Give us nothing but vegetables to eat and water to drink. Then compare our appearance with that of the young men who eat the royal food, and treat your servants in accordance with what you see." So he agreed to this and tested them for ten days.

At the end of the ten days they looked healthier and better nourished than any of the young men who ate the royal food. So the guard took away their choice food and the wine they were to drink and gave them vegetables instead.

To these four young men God gave knowledge and understanding of all kinds of literature and learning. And Daniel could understand visions and dreams of all kinds. (1:8–17)

About now you may be thinking, "What does it take to stick to a commitment like Daniel and his three friends did? Is there something I can buy, bid for, or invent to make that happen for me? Is this courage obtainable for everybody? Or does God select who gets this extra strength? How can I know this personally?"

The Promises

One thing is for sure, courage can't be purchased at some cheap drug store. It comes from the Lord, making it possible for anyone to know its power in their life. God loves to set us free from bondage, no matter what chains are around our necks. Just look at this:

> For God did not give us a spirit of timidity, but a spirit of power, of love and of self-discipline. (2 Timothy 1:7)

> But perfect love drives out fear . . . (1 John 4:18)

> I sought the LORD, and he answered me;
>   he delivered me from all my fears.
>   (Psalm 34:4)

The Plan

With those promises we need a plan to pass the tests that require courage. Looking closely at Daniel's words, we see the strategy he used.

First, there was purity in his heart. "Daniel resolved not to defile himself . . ." (1:8a). Even as a slave Daniel determined to have his heart set on honoring the Lord. The same is needed today. You can goof off in school, be the class clown, party your life away, and become a couch potato watching Madonna on MTV. Nothing special is needed for that. But having purity in your heart means there is a direct goal being set, and a plan of action is in

25

place. As runners keep their eyes on the tape at the finish line, so do those set on having purity in their hearts. Temptations may try to stop that race of purity, but with our eyes on the target of godliness, we won't get sidetracked. Daniel didn't, and we won't either.

Second, there is the security of having the Lord at our side. "Now God had caused the official to show favor and sympathy to Daniel" (1:9). What a tremendous truth! Even as a slave, Daniel knew God was with him. The Lord is with us also. Notice what He says:

> And surely I am with you always, to the very end of the age. (Matthew 28:20b)

> Never will I leave you;
>   never will I forsake you. (Hebrews 13:5b)

> If God is for us, who can be against us?
> (Romans 8:31b)

What security! Almighty God Himself states we are His and He is ours.

My friend Paul found this to be true after years of being enslaved to anger. He was mad at God for the death of his father. We spent hours talking, and always seemed to end at the same place; his wounded spirit was filled with more and more questions as to why God had allowed his father to die.

But when I saw him last summer at Mahaffey Bible Camp in Pennsylvania where I was speaking, he was different. After we talked, he shared with me something he had written. With his permission I share it with you.

WHY?

Oh God, please tell me this hasn't happened. Let this be merely my worst nightmare. This just can't be possible. How could You do this to me? It isn't fair God, it just isn't fair. It's my birthday; I'm finally a teenager, and now You have let this happen. Why?

BE STILL AND KNOW THAT I AM GOD. I ALONE AM GOD. MY WAYS ARE HIGHER THAN YOUR WAYS. I AM WHO I AM.

God this doesn't make sense. I loved him so much. He was always there for me, making sure that I had what I needed. He loved me, protected me, taught me, cared for me. Now he is gone, You have taken him from me. Is this some sort of a cruel joke? Why?

BE STILL AND KNOW THAT I AM GOD. I ALONE AM GOD. MY WAYS ARE HIGHER THAN YOUR WAYS. I AM WHO I AM.

God, he loved You. He lived his life for You. He brought me up to believe that You are good and loving. He served You with all his life, and now You have taken that life from him. You have killed my father. How can You be so cruel? How can You be so uncaring and heartless? Why?

BE STILL AND KNOW THAT I AM GOD. I ALONE AM GOD. MY WAYS ARE HIGHER

THAN YOUR WAYS. I AM WHO I AM.

God, I need him so much. Who will teach me to grow into a man? To whom will I turn to ask questions that sons ask fathers? I'm only 13; I'm too young to be the man of the house. I need my father to lean on. All my friends do things with their fathers. You didn't take them. Why?

BE STILL AND KNOW THAT I AM GOD. I ALONE AM GOD. MY WAYS ARE HIGHER THAN YOUR WAYS. I AM WHO I AM.

God, it's been 16 years now. I still don't understand. It just doesn't seem fair. I needed him when I was in trouble. I needed him when I went to college. I needed him when I got married. I needed him when my little girl was born. I needed him, but You took him away from me. Why?

BE STILL AND KNOW THAT I AM GOD. I ALONE AM GOD. MY WAYS ARE HIGHER THAN YOUR WAYS. I AM WHO I AM.

God, it is true I don't understand, but I stand here, still, and know that You are my God. You alone are God. Your ways are higher than my ways. You are Alpha and Omega, Lord God Almighty. Because You are, I no longer ask "Why?".

Even in the hardest time of his life, my friend Paul knew the security of the Lord. So did Daniel. So can you!

Third, Daniel is consistent. Notice Daniel 1:15: "At the end of the ten days they looked healthier and better nourished than any of the young men who ate the royal food." The perseverance of these teens was remarkable. Their endurance proved that the Lord was with them. Because of their tenacity, God could do greater things.

It takes courage to face some tests in life. Yet, the Lord declares He is with us. As we walk with Him in purity, He proves His adherence to us, no matter what. That is what brought Daniel and his three friends through. My friend Paul would affirm that as well.

What about you? Going through some tough times? Facing some hard tests in life? Don't cheat yourself out of seeing God do something tremendous in your life by taking the easy way out. Stand tall, and walk with God in purity. Allow Him to give you His security as you honor Him. He will bring you through. That's a promise. God specializes in making men and women into heroes as a result of tough times.

God Knows What He's About

When God wants to drill a man
    And thrill a man
    And skill a man,
When God wants to mold a man
    To play the noblest part;
When He yearns with all His heart
    To create so great and bold a man
That all the world may be amazed,
Watch His methods, watch His ways!

29

How He ruthlessly perfects
Whom He royally elects!
How He hammers him and hurts him
And with mighty blows converts him
Into trial shapes of clay which
Only God understands;
While his tortured heart is crying
And he lifts beseeching hands!
How He bends but never breaks
When his good He undertakes;
How He uses whom He chooses
And with every purpose fuses him;
By every act induces him
To try His splendor out—
God knows what He's about!

Author Unknown[1]

Putting It into My Life

1. What kind of test are you facing right now? Can it be measured by a grade, a jersey or a team listing? Who is passing out the grades for this exam?

2. What causes you to experience stress in your life? How well did you do on the stress test? What can you do to reduce your stress level? What seems to be your biggest concern? Do you think the Lord can handle the stress events in your life right now?

3. What is the most frightening thing you face? Do you know of anyone else who faced this situation? How did they handle it? How are you going

to face it tomorrow? Do you think the Lord has anything to say to you about it? What?

4. What would you say to Daniel if you had a chance to talk with him? How did he and his three friends handle becoming slaves as teenagers? Do you think they ever laid awake at night asking the Lord why this had happened to them?

5. What enslaves you now? Are you tired of those chains choking you and bruising your ankles? How can you get released? Do you think the Lord can pick the lock and set you free? Have you asked Him? What are His promises to those who are shackled? Does He mean it, or is He just joking?

3

Anger vs. Assurance

————————

Dreams really are strange sometimes, aren't they? Once when I was teaching school I had a weird one. In my dream, I was going to have to discipline a student. As I approached his desk, he began punching, kicking and shouting at me, demanding that I leave him alone. Becoming angry, I started punching him back. About that time, I was awakened by my wife screaming at me to wake up, and get off of her. When I "came to," I realized that I was not punching the student, but my wife! Poor Kay—she thought the Iraqis were attacking. I apologized and went back to sleep. For breakfast the next morning, I was served cold coffee, burnt toast, and an egg that resembled a hockey puck. That was the last time I had a dream like that!

What is the wildest dream you ever had? Isn't it

remarkable how real some dreams seem to be? Like when:

- You can't seem to run or even move when something or someone is chasing you in a dream.
- In a dream you are on a date that is a "dream come true" and your little brother or sister bursts through the bedroom door and jumps on your bed, waking you from the best part of the dream.
- A dream is so scary, you make a vow with yourself that you will never sleep again until you are 35.

The Bible tells of different people who had dreams. Jacob dreamed about a ladder descending from heaven (Genesis 28:10–22). Joseph dreamed his brothers would honor him as someone special (Genesis 37:5–11). Pharaoh also had a dream that he couldn't interpret. Only Joseph could give the meaning (Genesis 41). In the New Testament, Joseph, the earthly father of Jesus, had a dream about Mary and the baby she was carrying, who would be the Savior of the world (Matthew 1:18–24). Pilate's wife had a dream regarding the controversy over Christ; she warned Pilate to leave it alone (Matthew 27:19). So dreams are throughout Scripture. They serve as an important part of how God communicated to people.

In the Bible times, whenever an interpretation could not be given to a king or someone in authority, it sometimes caused them to experience a "Maalox moment." Daniel 2 records such a situation:

33

In the second year of his reign, Nebuchadnezzar had dreams; his mind was troubled and he
could not sleep. So the king summoned the
magicians, enchanters, sorcerers and astrologers
to tell him what he had dreamed. When they
came in and stood before the king, he said to
them, "I have had a dream that troubles me and I
want to know what it means."

Then the astrologers answered the king in
Aramaic, "O king, live forever! Tell your servants
the dream, and we will interpret it."

The king replied to the astrologers, "This is
what I have firmly decided: If you do not tell me
what my dream was and interpret it, I will have
you cut into pieces and your houses turned into
piles of rubble. But if you tell me the dream and
explain it, you will receive from me gifts and
rewards and great honor. So tell me the dream
and interpret it for me." (vv. 1–6)

Obviously, Nebuchadnezzar demands an answer.
He calls in the soothsayers, the sorcerers, and others
to do two things: 1) repeat what happened in the
dream, and 2) interpret it. He adds this warning:
failure to do so will result in these people becoming
history. Nice guy, huh?

Three times these soothsayers ask for the dream to
be told to them by the king, in an attempt to stall
for time. The king became so angry that he
demanded not only their death, but also the death
of Daniel and his three friends.

Look at this:

This made the king so angry and furious that he ordered the execution of all the wise men of Babylon. So the decree was issued to put the wise men to death, and men were sent to look for Daniel and his friends to put them to death. (2:12–13)

Apparently, King Nebuchadnezzar had never read "How to Win Sheepherders and Influence Camel Riders." His anger consumed him, making him irrational, bent on destruction, full of rage and bitterness. Have you ever met anyone like that?

As a pastor and worker with college people, I have seen people mad. Susan's anger quickly reached a boiling point when she talked about her dad's affair with another woman. Her chair vibrated the floor as her body shook in rage. The same was true of Tom. He was so mad at a friend for betraying a secret told in confidence he could hardly see straight. Ginger's anger toward her brother for running away caused her to weep, asking, "How could he be so insensitive, so uncaring and self-centered?" What a nightmare anger can be!

Anger comes in various stages. One writer explains:

Psychologists have noted that anger has at least five phases. First, there is "mild irritation"—a feeling of minor discomfort brought on by someone or something. Next comes "indignation"—frustration over something unfair or unreasonable. From there, indignation transitions into "wrath"—a strong desire to avenge or punish, which never goes unexpressed. Wrath then leads to "fury"—a state that suggests violence and temporary loss of control. Moving in to the last phase, the full moon of anger is "rage"—the most dangerous form, where acts of violence are committed by people scarcely aware of what they're doing. Like the father in a fit of jealous rage, brutally murdered five people . . . his sister-in-law, his wife, and his three children.[1]

Apparently, Nebuchadnezzar was at "stage five." He ordered the death of many, and his "hit list" included Daniel.

Confidence — A Trait of a Hero

What would you do if someone had ordered your death? Break out into a cold sweat? Think it was a bad dream? Cry? Become angry? Faint? Wet your pants? Notice Daniel's response in Daniel 2:14–16:

> When Arioch, the commander of the king's guard, had gone out to put to death the wise men of Babylon, Daniel spoke to him with wisdom and tact. He asked the king's officer, "Why did the king issue such a harsh decree?" Arioch then explained the matter to Daniel. At this, Daniel went in to the king and asked for time, so that he might interpret the dream for him.

What a hero! He responds with "wisdom and

tact." Assurance seems to be oozing out of our man. He doesn't scream, kick, punch, yell or start crying uncontrollably. He doesn't faint, and the Bible doesn't give a hint of him wetting his pants. It does say that Daniel praised God. Check it out:

Then Daniel returned to his house and explained the matter to his friends Hananiah, Mishael and Azariah. He urged them to plead for mercy from the God of heaven concerning this mystery, so that he and his friends might not be executed with the rest of the wise men of Babylon. During the night the mystery was revealed to Daniel in a vision. Then Daniel praised the God of heaven and said:

"Praise be to the name of God for ever
        and ever;
    wisdom and power are his.
He changes times and seasons;
    he sets up kings and deposes them.
He gives wisdom to the wise
    and knowledge to the discerning.
He reveals deep and hidden things;
    he knows what lies in darkness,
    and light dwells with him.
I thank and praise you, O God of my fathers;
    You have given me wisdom and power,
    you have made known to me what we
        asked of you,
    you have made known to us the
        dream of the king." (2:17–23)

37

Anchors for Assurance in Tough Times

Daniel's assurance is nothing short of amazing. Though innocent, his death is ordered. Yet, he is calm and aware of God's presence. What a role model, example and hero.

In another chapter, we will see how Daniel interpreted the dream, and how it became reality. But before we close this chapter, with Daniel on his knees, let's try to transfer his confidence to ourselves. How do teens do what he did with death staring him eyeball to eyeball? Can we have that same assurance? What was Daniel's secret? I think it can be nailed down in two ways.

1. God does His best work when we are weakest.

The Lord seems to prove this throughout Scripture, like when Joseph was in prison, or when Moses and Israel were at the Red Sea with Pharaoh's deadly posse hot on their heels. Joshua saw that at Jericho, and so did David, as a 17-year-old facing Goliath. God loves to prove who has the last word, and who is boss. As Chuck Swindoll observes:

> A lot of you who read this page are backed up against a set of circumstances that seem to spell T-H-E E-N-D. All looks almost hopeless. Pretty well finished. Apparently over. Maybe you need to read that again, underlining those words: "seem to" . . . "almost" . . . "pretty well" . . . "apparently."

Your adversary would love for you to assume the worst. He'd enjoy seeing you heave a sigh and resign yourself to depressed feelings that accompany defeat, failure, maximum resentment, and minimum faith. After all, it's fairly obvious you're through. Well . . . since when does "fairly obvious" draw the curtain on the last act? It's been my experience that when God is involved, anything can happen. The One who directed that stone in between Goliath's eyes and split the Red Sea down the middle and leveled that wall around Jericho and brought His Son back from beyond takes delight in mixing up the odds as He alters the obvious and bypasses the inevitable.[2]

Two soldiers who were Christians found that God does His best work when we are weakest. They were in boot camp with the weirdest guy they had ever met. Determined to share Christ with this recruit, they went to extremes in trying to win his friendship. However, no matter what these soldiers tried, they met resistance. Yet, at their weakest point, God broke through. Listen to this account as told by Christian comedian, Mike Warnke:

> I did everything I could to shut those guys up. Man, I tore up their Bibles. I punched them in the mouth. I knocked them down. I tore up their lockers. I made life hell for them for three months.
> And finally just before we got ready to leave

boot camp, this old boy came walking in the room, and he said, "Listen, I'm gonna tell you about Jesus." I jumped up and grabbed him by the front of his uniform and rared back and gave him a shove. And when I did he caught his foot on the edge of a locker and fell. And he spun around and tried to catch himself against this table, and he missed. And the edge of the table hit him right under the nose. I've never seen so much blood in one place. And the impact of his face hitting that table was so hard that it actually knocked him backwards on his back, and he hit the floor with a thud.

Blood splattered every place, blood running down his face, soaking into his shirt, blood running down the sides of his cheeks and into his ears and out onto the floor, blood soaking into his hair, blood everywhere.

And I walked out and looked at him laying on the floor, and I said, "You say Jesus to me again, just one more time, and I'll take a razor blade, and I'll open you up like a Christmas turkey."

And he looked up to me, with tears in his eyes and his eyes already starting to turn black and blue, and the blood gushing from his broken nose, and he said, "I've got to tell ya about Jesus, Mike, 'cause Jesus loves you."

I said, "Man, what are you doing this for?"

"Because I love you too."

I said, "You love me? You're laying there in a pool of your own blood from a broken nose that I gave you, and you're telling me you love me?"

I said, "Man, you're crazy!"

He said, "The only reason you say that is because you don't even know what love is."

I said, "Okay, smart guy, what's love?" And he reached up, and he wiped blood off the bottom of his face, and he held his hand out to me, and he said, "Mike, Jesus Christ hung on a cross, and He shed His blood for you, and if you're good enough for Jesus, man, you're good enough for me."[3]

What is the toughest situation you are facing? Your family? Your friends? Are anger and hatred eating you alive? Does fear have you by the throat? Let *God* take care of that like He did for those two soldiers who influenced Mike Warnke to come to Christ.

2. Prayer is the resource to meet your needs.

Isn't it interesting that Daniel didn't take a poll as to what he should do? His life was being threatened. He didn't try to wiggle his way out. Nothing is mentioned about him "making a deal" with God—you know—the old, *"God get me out of this one and I'll do anything go anywhere and be what you want me to be"* prayer. Not Daniel. He honors God, and prays. Confidently he goes to the One with the answers. What a hero! It's like the old saying goes: "Knees don't knock when you kneel on them!"

This is proven in Scripture.

And I will do whatever you ask in my name, so

that the Son may bring glory to the Father. You may ask me for anything in my name, and I will do it. (John 14:13–14)

And receive from him anything we ask, because we obey his commands and do what pleases him. (1 John 3:22)

If you believe, you will receive whatever you ask for in prayer. (Matthew 21:22)

Know that the LORD has set apart the
  godly for himself;
    the LORD will hear when I call to Him.
      (Psalm 4:3)

Then you will call upon me and come and pray to me, and I will listen to you. (Jeremiah 29:12)

Call to me and I will answer you and tell you great and unsearchable things you do not know. (33:3)

What a great God Daniel served. We serve the same One who proves His best work at our weakest points, and fulfills His promise of prayer being the resource to meet our needs. And that's no nightmare—that's a dream come true, and a powerful reality. I think Mike Warnke would agree, don't you?

Have you talked with God today?

Putting It into My Life

1. What do you dream about most often? Is it scary? Funny? Sad? Stupid?

2. How would you feel if you were Daniel, and your immediate death sentence had been given? What would you do? Freak out? Be confident? Faint?

3. What is the closest you have ever been to death? Was your reaction surprising? What were your thoughts as you thought about your life ending?

4. Has God ever proven He does His finest work when you are at your weakest point? What happened? How has that affected you? Can you ever be the same?

5. Have you ever seen how prayer is the resource to meet your needs? Have you ever tried that personally? Did it work? What happened? Were you or someone near you changed?

6. React to this statement: "Knees don't knock when you kneel on them!" Do you believe that? Is that just for preachers, women and retired people? Do you think God could do that in your life? How? Will you try it today?

4

Prayer—The Power of Heroes

O lympic gold medalist Eric Liddell was a mighty hero and winner. The movie *Chariots of Fire* portrayed his life. But Liddell had another life outside the track and field events of world competition. In fact, he was a prisoner of war at Weinsen Camp in North China during World War II.

You may be asking what he was like in that context. Was he brave? A cry-baby? A milquetoast? Joyful? One lady who was in the same prison camp with Liddell reported this:

> What was his secret? Once I asked him, but I really knew already, for my husband was in his dormitory and shared the secret with him. Every morning about 6 a.m., with curtains tightly drawn to keep in the shining of our peanut-oil

lamp, lest the prowling sentries would think someone was trying to escape, he used to climb out of his top bunk, past the sleeping forms of his mates. Then, at the small Chinese table, the two men would sit close together with the light just enough to illuminate their Bibles and notebooks. Silently, they read, prayed, thought about what should be done. Eric was a man of prayer not only at set times—though he did not like to miss a prayer meeting or communion service when such could be arranged. He talked to God all the time, naturally, as one can who enters the "School of Prayer" to learn this way of inner discipline. He seemed to have no weighty mental problems: his life was grounded in God, in faith, and in trust.[1]

What a hero Eric Liddell was! He had real power for real living!

Unfortunately, we have been sold a lot of junk about prayer. We have been told that prayer:

- is "okay," but don't get too excited about it.
- is for the weak, insecure, and "unstable." No "real" man or woman needs to pray.
- should be banned from school.
- works only if you are "good."

What a bunch of trash! It is prayer that changes things and makes people winners and mighty warriors! Any wimp can sit on his fanny, twiddling his thumbs and doing nothing. It takes real power to go to God's throne and petition His majesty!

Tony Campolo is a fervent believer in prayer. He had an unusual experience once that was a direct result of prayer. As he tells it, he was invited to preach in a chapel service of a Christian college. Before the service several people were praying for him. One man in particular got a little carried away when it was his turn to pray. Listen to what happened next:

> One guy wasn't even praying for me. Instead he went on and on praying for somebody named Charlie Stoltzfus. "Dear Lord," he shouted, "You know Charlie Stoltzfus. He lives in that silver trailer down the road about a mile. You know the trailer, Lord, just down the road on the right-hand side." I felt like saying, "Knock it off, fella, what do you think God's doing? Saying, 'What's the address again?'"
>
> Anyway, he went on and on and on: "Lord, Charlie told me this morning that he's decided to leave his wife and three kids. He told me that he was walking out on his family. Lord, step in, do something, bring the people in that family back together again!"
>
> All the while, I'm kneeling there with eight guys leaning on my head and I'm asking myself, "When's this guy going to knock it off so I can get these Pentecostal preachers off my head?" But he kept going on and on about Charlie Stoltzfus' leaving his wife and kids, giving God constant reminders that he lived in a silver trailer a mile

down the road on the right-hand side.

Finally, the prayers were over and I went into the pulpit and preached. After I was finished, I got in my car, drove to the Pennsylvania Turnpike, and headed for home.

As I drove onto the turnpike, I noticed a hitchhiker. Now, I know you're not supposed to pick them up, but I'm a preacher and whenever I can get anybody locked in as a captive audience, I do it. So, I stopped and picked him up. We drove a few minutes and I said, "Hi, my name's Tony Campolo. What's your name?" He said, "My name is Charlie Stoltzfus." I couldn't believe it!

I got off the turnpike at the next exit and headed back. He got a bit uneasy with that and after a few minutes he said, "Hey, mister, where are you taking me?" I said, "I'm taking you home." He narrowed his eyes and asked, "Why?"

I said, "Because you just left your wife and three children, right?" That blew him away. "Yeah! Yeah, that's right." With shock written all over his face, he plastered himself against the car door and never took his eyes off me.

I drove off the turnpike at the next exit. Then I really did him in as I drove right to his silver trailer. When I pulled up, his eyes seemed to bulge as he asked, "How did you know that I lived here?" I said, "God told me." (I believe God did tell me.)

We got out of the car and I ordered him to get in that trailer. Half shaking he answered, "Right mister, sure! Sure! I'm going."

When he opened the trailer door his wife exclaimed, "You're back! You're back!" He whispered in her ear and the more he talked, the bigger her eyes got.

Then I said with real authority, "The two of you sit down. I'm going to talk and you two are going to listen!" Man! Did they listen! I mean, I was like E.F. Hutton!

That afternoon I led those two young people to Jesus Christ. And today, that guy is a preacher of the gospel out in California.[2]

Like Eric Liddell and Tony Campolo, Daniel believed in prayer too. That is why he is a hero. When we left him in the last chapter, Daniel was in a life-threatening situation. The king was about to kill everyone in sight for not having his dream told as well as interpreted for him. However, Daniel, a foreign slave, asks for permission to address the king. He isn't afraid. Why should he be? After all, he has already addressed the King of kings in prayer! What was this earthly king to him?

The king asked Daniel (also called Belteshazzar) "Are you able to tell me what I saw in my dream and interpret it?"

Daniel replied, "No wise man, enchanter, magician or diviner can explain to the king the mystery he has asked about, but there is a God in heaven who reveals mysteries. He has shown King Nebuchadnezzar what will happen in the days to come. Your dream and the visions that passed through your mind as you lay on your bed are these:

"As you were lying there, O king, your mind turned to things to come, and the revealer of mysteries showed you what is going to happen. As for me, this mystery has been revealed to me, not because I have greater wisdom than other living men, but so that you, O king, may know the interpretation and that you may understand what went through your mind." (2:26–30)

Right on, Daniel! This teenager "rang the bell." Not only did he tell the king the dream, but he also gave the interpretation. Was that not impressive? Nebuchadnezzar sure was convinced. Here's the proof:

Then King Nebuchadnezzar fell prostrate before Daniel and paid him honor and ordered that an offering and incense be presented to him. The king said to Daniel, "Surely your God is the God of gods and the Lord of kings and a revealer of mysteries, for you were able to reveal this mystery."

Then the king placed Daniel in a high position and lavished many gifts on him. He made him ruler over the entire province of Babylon and placed him in charge of all its wise men. Moreover, at Daniel's request the king appointed Shadrach, Meshach and Abednego administrators over the province of Babylon, while Daniel himself remained at the royal court. (2:46–49)

Can't you see it? The king falling face-first in front of this teenage slave boy! No one on earth was more powerful than Nebuchadnezzar then. And no one was more impressed with one single teenager than the king. He literally collapsed at his feet. Wow!

A Call from the President

Today that would be like sitting in history class, and your name is called over the loudspeaker. "Please come to the office." Nervously, you walk in, and are handed the telephone. "Hello. This is who? Mr. President! Can I come where, sir? Well, yes, I can come to the White House if you send a helicopter to pick me up and fly me to the White House." A few minutes later, a chopper lands on the football field of your high school to pick you up. All your friends are looking out the windows of the classrooms in disbelief. Some are clapping, some are waving, and others are so stunned they are just standing there with their bare faces hanging out. Meanwhile all of your teachers are saying to one another; "I knew one day, he would be great. He always was my favorite student."

Then the pilot lifts off and flies you to Washington, D.C. You walk into the Oval Office, and the president salutes. After talking about world problems, he is so amazed at your knowledge and insights, he literally lays face first on the carpet at your feet, and volunteers to polish up your "scuffed-up" Reeboks!

In essence, that is what happened to Daniel. Incredible! And remember, he was only a teenager! How did Daniel have the skill to know what the king had dreamed? Did a palm reader tell him? Was he informed by playing a special card game? Had he tinkered with Dungeons & Dragons? No way! One word tells how Daniel knew what was happening: prayer. It works. It is not boring, dry, dusty, a waste of time or something old ladies do. It is the very power of God that changes people, events and lives, and gives direction for today. It is calling on Almighty God and finding His way best for life.

There are some people who try to discredit prayer, claiming it is not a science that can be measured, put on a slide and looked at under a microscope or placed in a test tube. Dr. Richard Harvey, a famous preacher, tells about a professor who refused to believe in a God who answered prayer. The professor's name was Dr. Lee.

Dr. Lee was a very influential man, who had received many honors for his work. However, he could not accept the idea that God would intervene in a person's life. In fact, in one of his lectures, given every year, he would mock the possibility of prayer being real. Dr. Harvey tells it this way:

> Dr. Lee's third lecture was on the subject of the impossibility of an objective answer to prayer. He said he would prove his contention. At the end of his lecture he announced that he would step down from his platform onto the concrete floor. Then he would challenge, "Is there anybody here who still believes in prayer?" And he would say, "Before you answer, let me tell you what I am going to do and what I am going to

ask you to do. I will turn around, take a glass flask and hold it at arm's length." Then he would continue, "If you believe that God answers prayer, I want you to stand and pray that when I drop this flask, it won't break. I want you to know that your prayers and the prayers of your parents and Sunday School teachers, and even the prayers of your own pastor cannot prevent this flask from breaking. If you wish to have them here we will put this off until you return after the Thanksgiving recess."

No one had ever accepted Dr. Lee's challenge. But one year a certain freshman learned about Dr. Lee's dare. And decided prayerfully that he would accept the challenge. He believed that God had given him the promise, ". . . if two of you shall agree on earth as touching any thing that they shall ask, it shall be done for them by my Father, who is in heaven." Then the young man sought out another Christian to stand with him in prayer for courage and faith and they believed together that God would keep the flask from breaking.

The day came. At the end of the final lecture on prayer, the annual challenge was put forth as it had been for 12 years. As soon as Dr. Lee asked, "Is there anyone here who believes God answers prayer?" the young man stepped into the aisle and raised his hand and said, "Dr. Lee, I do."

"Well, this is most interesting. But young man, you had better let me explain what I am going to do and then we'll see if you still desire to pray. I wouldn't want you to be embarrassed before this class."

The professor then took the glass flask and held it out in front of him over the cement floor. "Now I ask you to pray—if you still want to do it—that this flask won't break. After you pray, I'll drop it and I can assure you that it will hit the cement floor and break into hundreds of pieces, and that no prayer can prevent it. Do you still want to pray?"

"Yes, Dr. Lee, I do."

"Well," said the professor, "this is most interesting." And turning to the class he said sarcastically, "Now we will be most reverent while this young man prays." Then he turned to the young man, "Now you may pray."

The freshman just lifted his countenance toward heaven and prayed, "God, I know that you hear me. Please honor the name of your Son, Jesus Christ, and honor me, your servant. Don't let the flask break. Amen."

Dr. Lee stretched his arm out as far as he could, opened his hand and let the flask fall. It fell in an arc, hit the toe of Dr. Lee's shoe, rolled over and did not break. There was no movement of air and there were no open windows. The class whistled, clapped and shouted. And Dr. Lee ceased his annual lectures against prayer.[3]

Right on! What a hero this freshman was to stand up against the professor. He was a witness that God is alive and well and full of answers to prayer!

I remember two key times when God answered my prayers. Though there have been dozens of similar events, allow these two to be building blocks for you.

Needed: A Guitar

In college I took guitar lessons, and was advancing well. I had borrowed a guitar from a friend for a year, but had to return it before summer break.

I remembered various promises in Scripture about asking and receiving, so I decided to go for it. My prayer was something like this:

"Lord, I would like a guitar, but not just any guitar. Lord, I would like a *Martin* guitar. As I receive it, Lord, I promise to play for your glory. Thank you."

Praying for a *Martin* guitar would be like asking for a Steinway piano. It would be like wanting not just a car, but a 300 ZX. A Martin is the best acoustic guitar, and my heart was set on one.

One afternoon two weeks later, a friend knocked on my dorm room door, came in and said this: "Les, two weeks ago God impressed on me to give you this guitar. I've never done anything like this, but here you are. Its yours, free. And by the way, its a Martin." Praise the Lord!

A Teen Transformed

Another time of answered prayer came one summer while I was speaking at Delta Lake Bible Conference Center in New York State. A teen there was obviously angry, bitter and full of hatred toward his mom. He cussed and kicked and acted like a real jerk all the way to the camp. "I hate this camp," he said. "When I get home, I'm going to look into becoming a Satanist."

Later that week, several people gathered for prayer and fasting during the noon hour. We prayed God would show this teen his sin and his need for Jesus, and cause him to repent.

That very night at camp, when the invitation was given at the end of the sermon, that 15-year-old teenager ran to the altar where he knelt and prayed to receive Jesus as his Savior. The next night an invitation was given for people to surrender their lives to full-time Christian service. Again, this once-angry, bitter teenager accepted God's offer and bowed his knee to Christian ministry as the Lord would lead him. Hallelujah!

Daniel discovered prayer could change things. So did Eric Liddell and a college freshman. It is amazing the difference it makes in a life.

A youth group in Traverse City, Michigan discovered this truth as well:

Intercessors for America newsletter (January 1976) contained the following exciting account: Christians from Traverse City, Michigan, were united in prayer, claiming that God was going to stop the "glitter rock band" KISS from performing, as the band openly calls on demons during their concerts. The young believers even told their classmates the KISS concert would not happen. Many Christians were praying behind the scenes the very moment the concert was to begin. Six thousand young people (average age 16 to 17 years old) showed up at the Glacier Dome concert hall. Many of them knew Christians were praying against the concert. *Coincidentally* twelve thousand dollars' worth of the band's electronic equipment blew up! After an hour of attempted repair work, the crowd was turned away. No concert in answer to prayer.[4]

Now we're talking! (Or, more like, now we're praying!)

How Can I Get Started?

You may be asking: "How can I know that kind of power? Do you have to be 'Super-spiritual Sam or Susie' to be able to get answers like this?" I have found that to have power in prayer the following is necessary:

1. Consistency

The "hit-and-miss" stuff doesn't make it. You would not show up at the game after missing practice all week, and expect to be ready for the competition, would you? How ridiculous! Without consistency and dedication to the sport, you cannot be at maximum performance. The same is true with prayer. Unless consistency is a part of your plan for prayer, forget it. You are disqualified because you don't understand the rules.

2. Develop a Pattern

Just as you might use a map on a trip to make sure you are following the right road, patterns for prayer are needed to guide you to a consistent, powerful prayer life. Without such patterns, you can lose interest, make wrong turns, and yawn your way through a journey that could be phenomenal!

Here's an idea I have used with different youth groups that I've never seen fail. Get an ordinary shoe box and a pack of 3x5 cards. On the cards, write out prayer requests and date them. Make a sign and put it on the box that says: "The Devil Can Eat Dirt!" As prayers are answered, put them in the box. When the devil starts to tell you prayer is boring, a drag, and a waste of time, point to the box and declare: "Eat dirt, Devil! I serve a prayer-answering, power-giving God!"

3. Dismiss the "Earning Points" Idea

God doesn't give out "points." He does reward those who seek Him and is pleased when we come to Him in prayer. But the idea that we can "score" with God because we are "good boys and girls" by praying every day is totally foreign to Scripture. Jack Hayford, a pastor in California, explains:

> Contrary to many people's ideas, prayer is not another kind of work. While there is a ministry of prayer, it is not a means by which you earn points with God or a fleshly attempt to gain God's attention or favor through your human effort. Getting God to restore His image in you is

not a reward He gives in response to a certain quantity of prayer. God is not looking down condescendingly, watching to see when you have bowed and scraped enough to receive a holy fortune cookie, an ego-stroking pat on the head or a paternal smile. Prayer is not a works program.

But prayer does enter strongly into the development of my relationship with God:

• In prayer I come to learn more about God's person
• In so doing I will discover the beginning of His nature infusing my nature with His
• I will find healing in His presence
• I discover self-understanding while with Him, as
• I search my own heart, my own motives and my own thoughts.

I best learn about Him before His Throne and I best learn about me while I'm with Him. Time in His presence, therefore, is not earning time, it's learning time.[5]

Get the idea? Prayer is meeting God, and Him meeting us. The result is things are done that can only be accomplished by the Holy Spirit, like a teenager astonishing a king by telling and interpreting the dream of the monarch.

Take the challenge—become a person of prayer, and allow the Lord to change you, your world and people who are looking for answers. Daniel did. So did a world-class champion Eric Liddell, youth speaker Tony Campolo and a youth group in Michigan. Don't be afraid to take God at His word. Become a hero—from the knees up!

Putting It into My Life:

1. Have you ever been a part of a prayer meeting where things happened? What was the difference? How did it change you? Could you say you became more interested in prayer?

2. What do you think of Eric Liddell? Why was he so different even in a prison camp? Have you ever known the joy, desire and power he had? Do you think they could ever be a part of your everyday life? Have you asked for them?

3. Why was Daniel different than the normal high-schooler? Did you see his courage? Where did it come from? Would you like to be as bold as he was?

4. Suppose you *did* get a call from the Oval Office. Describe the feelings you would have.

5. When you pray, do you pray specifically or generally? Do you think God is impressed? Do you feel you need to impress Him? What does it take to "get through" to God?

6. Do you suppose you and your youth group could pray so intensely that a rock concert could be shut down? Have you ever wanted to be a part of something like that? How do you think it could happen?

5

Cool Men in a Hot Place

What influences you the most? Television? Music? How about advertisements like, "Sometimes you gotta break the rules," "Just do it!," "Just say no," "It's the right beer now"? Has a speech or sermon ever made a difference in you?

Who makes an impact on you? Your parents? A coach? Teachers? Youth pastors or sponsors? What about an aunt or uncle? Brother or sister? Maybe a neighbor? How about your friends?

Of all the advertisements, people and situations that we encounter, our friends have the greatest pull in our lives. More time is spent with them at school, at practices, in sports, eating lunch in the cafeteria, watching videos or just goofing off. Friends are important because often our identity and how we are perceived by others is found in who our friends are.

Let's face it: friends, like heroes, can have a negative or positive effect on us. In *Pulling Weeds,* I wrote about peer pressure and how it works:

Alice found she had some helpful friends. Alice had a problem with her temper. To put it bluntly, she was "bullheaded" and even mean at times. She hated these things in her life and genuinely wanted to be different. While at a retreat one summer, she sensed the Lord speaking to her about her temper. Several of her close friends prayed with her about her attitude. God used these friends as a good influence in Alice's life that week. So, in this instance, peer pressure was helpful.

Being a teenager and a positive, godly influence on your friends is not easy. The pressure to swear, tell bad jokes and be sexually active is powerful. It has smothered many teens. Coping with this kind of pressure is a tough fight, and the opponents have often delivered knock-out punches. This past summer, I heard about just such an incident.

A group of kids were bored one Friday night, so they thought they would have some fun. With a particular country road outside of town in mind, they devised a prank. They covered the center line on the road with dirt and painted a fake center line that veered off in the opposite direction. Then they hid by the side of the road to see what would happen.

It was a foggy night, and a school bus bringing the ball team home from an out-of-town game came down the road. The bus driver was not familiar with the road, so when he came to the part "adjusted" by these teens, he followed the new markings. The bus went off the road and plunged over a cliff, killing the entire team.[1]

It is amazing how people make a difference in us. They often are "makers" or "breakers" in our lives. Who is your best friend? Can you think what it would be like without him or her? How does this person influence you the most?

Being a friend involves many things. It means having fun at ball games, meeting at the mall, going camping or just talking. Being friends also means being affirmed by one another. Sara encouraged Marie to come to the play try-outs, giving her confidence in spite of Marie's nervousness. Sure enough, Marie got the part, and is grateful for Sara's encouragement. That is called partnership. I have a friend like that. When I am needing a boost, I call him up and usually inside of ten minutes, I am encouraged. He and I are partners, like two draft horses in a harness. When friends pull together, it is incredible what energy is found.

Occasionally a friend has to rebuke. That is never easy, as Jerry found out. He and Allen had been friends since tenth grade, attended camps and church together, and even double-dated to the movies. Jerry went to Allen after he had noticed Allen's language getting trashy. Without being "Holy

Joe," Jerry waited for a good time to talk to Allen. Though it wasn't easy to be confronted, Allen knew Jerry was right, and asked for forgiveness. To this day Allen is thankful for a friend like Jerry who cared enough to address the issue. Today they remain best of friends.

Being a friend means having fun, being open, having an honest relationship and building up one another. But it also means going through hard times together. Encouragement of friends during difficult times is invaluable. It is then that friendships are fastened down tight even when it is not easy.

Friends Facing Foes

Like anyone else, Daniel needed friends to lean on, to stand with him in tough times. He realized he could not excel in his relationship with the Lord without them. They made a direct impact on him. Though their names were peculiar (Shadrach, Meshach and Abednego), their friendship was a priority. Like a team of mountain climbers working as a unit, realizing one wrong move could result in death, Daniel and his friends knew they had to support one another to keep others from falling spiritually. It was as though each was roped together to rescue the other if he started slipping downward. Friends do that.

We aren't told when Nebuchadnezzar built it or what it looked like, but Daniel 3 says he had "an image of gold, ninety feet high and nine feet wide" (v. 1). He invited everyone to come to the dedication of this structure and offered this warning:

Then the herald loudly proclaimed, "This is what you are commanded to do, O peoples, nations and men of every language: As soon as you hear the sound of the horn, flute, zither, lyre, harp, pipes and all kinds of music, you must fall down and worship the image of gold that King Nebuchadnezzar has set up. Whoever does not fall down and worship will immediately be thrown into a blazing furnace." (vv. 4–6)

Can you imagine being told: "Worship this eight-story structure when the horn blows or you are burned biscuits"? No options—the royal edict was given: "bow or burn."

Images in Our Day

We don't have to look far in our society to see images erected tall, commanding our attention. People bow to them all the time, trying to drag others into the dirt with them. Here's what I mean:

Music: Teens often have a weak value system because of what they pour into their brains. When the horns of godless music blow, they bow down and get cooked in the coals of music that reduce them to ash.

Immorality: This idol seems to be adding additional floors to its structure daily. Though the building looks good, it is on shifting sand and will eventually crumble a life every time.

Lack of Honor: Seldom is respect for adults a virtue seen today, maybe because the old folks can't stay in step with the tune the world is playing. One thing is for sure though—you can't march to that tune forever without getting winded, needing a break, or getting old. Guess who won't be respected then?

Cheating: Cheating resembles the image Nebuchadnezzar had built—golden, shiny, and attractive. People bow to it thinking they are really safe. However, just as going inside the furnace would result in unbearable heat, entering the world of cheating assures scorching and permanent damage.

Fortunately, not everyone bows to these false images of our day. Teens everywhere are finding friends who can offer them hope and support. Alycia has decided to make a positive choice to listen to music that doesn't cook her convictions. Jordan has recommitted himself to moral purity rather than build wobbly sexual values on shifting sand. Clarissa is willing to honor her parents by slowing down her schedule and spending time at home. She is seeing more and more how her family is important to her. Brandon, though tempted to cheat on his time card at work, has committed himself to honesty. While the extra money he could be making by cheating looks "shiny" and attractive, he refuses to have his testimony scorched by a lack of integrity.

These decisions require gut-level commitment, but the privilege of walking God's way is worth it. And let's be honest—getting yourself "barbecued" by following the wrong crowd takes considerable commitment as well. But are you willing to make the right choice for the Lord? If you do, he will support you even when no one else is around.

Shadrach, Meshach and Abednego found that to be true:

> Shadrach, Meshach and Abednego replied to the king, "O Nebuchadnezzar, we do not need to defend ourselves before you in this matter. If we are thrown into the blazing furnace, the God we serve is able to save us from it, and he will rescue us from your hand, O king. But even if he does not, we want you to know, O king, that we will not serve your gods or worship the image of gold you have set up." (vv. 16–18)

What incredible courage these three gained through the strength of their relationship! What we find is a model of true friendship even when the heat was turned up, literally. Bonded together, these three teens were saying, "We will honor God, who is able to deliver us. But if he chooses not to, we still refuse to bow to you. So hang it on your beak, king!"

Do you remember the five stages of anger already mentioned? Without a doubt, King Nebuchadnezzar was again at stage five—fury. Notice this:

> Then Nebuchadnezzar was furious with Shadrach, Meshach and Abednego, and his attitude toward them changed. He ordered the furnace heated seven times hotter than usual and commanded some of the strongest soldiers in his army to tie up Shadrach, Meshach and Abednego and throw them into the blazing furnace. So

these men, wearing their robes, trousers, turbans and other clothes, were bound and thrown into the blazing furnace. (vv. 19–21)

Incredible! He was so angry, he had the furnace heated seven times hotter than usual, assuring the execution of these three friends. In fact, as Shadrach, Meshach and Abednego tumbled into this human oven, the soldiers who shoved them in were torched right on the spot.

Can you imagine what Shadrach, Meshach and Abednego were thinking as they were being taken to the furnace? They must have been saying, "This is the last roundup! My life is about to end right now." Yet in the face of death, with people literally dropping dead all around them, they refused to bow to a false god.

In case you're wondering if God was concerned, look how God honored their bravery.

> Then King Nebuchadnezzar leaped to his feet in amazement and asked his advisers, "Weren't there three men that we tied up and threw into the fire?"
>
> They replied, "Certainly, O king."
>
> He said, "Look! I see four men walking around in the fire, unbound and unharmed, and the fourth looks like a son of the gods." (vv. 24–25)

The Scripture goes on to say that the teenagers climbed out of the flames and the government officials crowded around them. After a thorough inspection the officials observed:

- the fire had not harmed their bodies
- not a hair was singed
- their robes were not scorched
- not even the smell of fire was on them.

Wow! God honors teens who refuse to bow to any other god.

There may be times when you have to "take it on the chops" for honoring God as Shadrach, Meshach, and Abednego did. I can assure you, however, God will honor your courage. Fred Hartley tells of one teen who learned that:

Not long ago my phone rang. It was Barbara. "What's wrong?" I could tell by her voice she had been crying.

"Fred, I feel like such a failure." She explained, "You see, I took your books to school, and I was reading them in study hall. First, the girl in front of me borrowed one; then two girls on the other side borrowed the others. When they started asking me all sorts of questions about God and heaven and my faith, I started to get all excited. The teacher told us to be quiet, but they kept talking about what they were reading. Finally the teacher came over—oh, Fred . . ."

She cried and then continued.

"He read the titles out loud and teased me, asking me to tell him where some Bible verse was found, which I didn't know. So everyone laughed at me, and he told me I couldn't be a Christian, since I didn't know the reference. When he sat down, they teased me, and they threw the books at me and called me names. It was awful.

"I tried to pray, but I couldn't, so I wrote out a prayer on a piece of paper. Then the teacher came over and read the prayer I had written— out loud to the whole class. I just felt terrible; I wanted to crawl out the window. Oh, Fred, what do I do? Did I blow it?"

"Barb, you now know better than before what it means to follow Jesus." Then I read her these words of Jesus, "Blessed are you when men revile you and persecute you and utter all kinds of evil against you falsely on my account. Rejoice and be glad, for your reward is great in heaven, for so men persecuted the prophets who were before you" (Matthew 5:11,12). Then I added, "In some special way, I know God will honor you for this. Just think, you might have been the only high-school kid in the state of Florida today to get mocked for following Jesus."

I don't think she was impressed with my sermonette. She was hurt. But she hung in there. She didn't fully understand what was happening, but she trusted God to work things out.

Four weeks ago one of the friends who laughed at Barb in the study hall came to church with her. That morning she prayed with Barb, and gave her life to Jesus. Perhaps Barb lost a few temporary friends, but at least one girl will be in heaven for all eternity.

Sure it's risky to follow Jesus, but it is the only way to live.[2]

Notice what God's Word says about Shadrach, Meshach and Abednego:

Then Nebuchadnezzar said, "Praise be to the God of Shadrach, Meshach and Abednego, who has sent his angel and rescued his servants! They trusted in him and defied the king's command and were willing to give up their lives rather than serve or worship any god except their own God. Therefore I decree that the people of any nation or language who say anything against the God of Shadrach, Meshach and Abednego be cut into pieces and their houses be turned into piles of rubble, for no other god can save in this way."

Then the king promoted Shadrach, Meshach and Abednego in the province of Babylon. (vv. 28–30)

This story of bravery and courage reminds me of the kite—it only rises when it is against the wind. These three had their friendship to strengthen them as they rose up against the threat of their lives. That's the way friends are. They support, stand alongside and affirm each other. Most importantly, they keep us on track with the Lord, even when the "heat gets turned up." In the end, we are glad they did.

You — A Friend of a King

The Bible talks about friends. Proverbs 17:17 tells

us "a friend loves at all times," and Proverbs 18:24 says, "there is a friend who sticks closer than a brother." Hours before Jesus was arrested He told the disciples, "I no longer call you servants . . . Instead I have called you friends" (John 15:15). What an honor to be known by royalty, for Jesus is the King of kings! He understands when we struggle. He has gone through persecution, temptation, and the heartache of being mistreated for honoring God. If you are hurting now, ask this Friend to comfort and encourage you with these truths:

> For everyone born of God overcomes the world. This is the victory that has overcome the world, even our faith. Who is it that overcomes the world? Only he who believes that Jesus is the Son of God. (1 John 5:4–5)

> So do not throw away your confidence; it will be richly rewarded. You need to persevere so that when you have done the will of God, you will receive what he has promised. (Hebrews 10:35–36)

> He who overcomes will, like them, be dressed in white. I will never blot out his name from the book of life, but will acknowledge his name before my Father and his angels. (Revelation 3:5)

> For God did not give us a spirit of timidity, but a spirit of power, of love and of self-discipline. (2 Timothy 1:7)

I consider that our present sufferings are not worth comparing with the glory that will be revealed in us. . . . For I am convinced that neither death nor life, neither angels nor demons, neither the present nor the future, nor any powers, neither height nor depth, nor anything else in all creation, will be able to separate us from the love of God that is in Christ Jesus our Lord. (Romans 8:18, 38–39)

Stay with this friend Jesus. He will stay with you, no matter what. That's a promise you can hang on to, no matter how hot the heat gets! Just ask Shadrach, Meshach and Abednego!

Putting It into My Life

1. What *is* the most significant influence in your life? Is it worth it? How long has it been a part of you?
2. What will be its effect on your life in six months? A year? Five years?
3. If you could write a letter to those three teens who caused the bus to go over the cliff, what would you say? Have you ever done something stupid like that? Who gave you the idea?
4. What should a friend be like? Are you a friend who encourages others like Sara did Marie? Could you ever confront a friend, like Jerry did Allen? Why or why not?
5. What are some images today that affect your friends? Would it take courage not to bow down to them? Are you helping some not to bow down now?

6. If you were a reporter and had a chance to interview Shadrach, Meshach and Abednego before going into the furnace, what would you ask them? What would you ask them after they came out?

7. Who do you think that fourth person was in the furnace? Do you have a friend who would stay with you like that? What is *His* name?

6

Pride vs. Passion

John F. Kennedy was served a big slice of humble pie while he was President. While concluding his speech at the Berlin Wall in 1963 he tried to say: "I too am a Berliner." However, in the German language there is another word that is very similar to "Berliner," but has a completely different meaning. Wouldn't you know it, President Kennedy used that word accidentally. Imagine the shock of the German people when the President concluded his very moving speech that went out around the world with these final remarks: "I too am a jelly donut!"

When "humble pie" is served to us in times like that it is enough to make us gag. It can't be washed down with anything but a big glass of "acceptance." Have you ever been humbled? I mean really reduced so much that you doubted your recovery?

Wasn't it embarrassing?

Sandra was mortified one day in the gym. As she was walking down the bleachers, the heel on her shoe got caught in a crack of a step. Before she knew it, she was rolling head first, eventually landing on the basketball court. As though falling on her face in front of 1,000 people wasn't humbling enough, she then discovered her skirt was up around her shoulders and over her head! The worst part came when those around were so shocked, they didn't know what to do. Consequently, they did nothing. No one moved. They simply stood there looking at her with all of her modesty being exposed for the rest of the world to see. Sandra's dignity vanished in front of the whole student body. She hasn't fully recovered yet!

I got humbled when I was 18, and of all times it happened when I was with about 85 other people. For graduation from high school, my parents gave me a trip to Europe. A Christian group called Spinning Spokes from Miami took teens every year on a tour throughout Europe on bicycles. There were 40 guys and 45 girls on my tour. I have never forgotten some of the things I learned about myself while on that trip.

First, I discovered that I was not "Mr. Marvelous Athlete." This realization came when I faced my first mountain in Belgium. Growing up in Florida, the highest mound I had ever seen was a sand pit on a golf course. While on European mountains that first week, pumping my pedals with all my might, I soon found out who was boss of the bike. It wasn't me.

Later on the tour, I also discovered I was not "Mr. Iron Stomach" either. This revelation came after I had some bad water in Germany. By the time we pedaled into Holland, I was a sick puppy. For three days I had the "10-yard dash." That was not exactly my idea of how to impress 45 female athletes. I was so ill, I was willing to do anything to feel better. I promised God I would scale the highest mountain, go to the darkest place in Africa, or swim the deepest ocean while preaching the gospel, if only I could get well. I was miserable! It was tough enough to be camping in tents, but we also rode a 10-speed every where we went. That was "exciting," for my biggest concern was not "How much further to Waterloo?" or "Is Anne Frank's house nearby?" but rather, "Where is the nearest rest room?"

While getting humbled can be crushing, it does serve a purpose. It reminds us of our limitations. Keith, a guy I was in high school with, discovered this the hard way.

It happened when he was streaking (running naked) down the school hall. While looking over his shoulder waving at the astonished classmates sticking their heads out of the doorways in disbelief, he was in his glory. All of a sudden, POW! Not looking where he was going, he ran right into the head football coach/dean of men of the high school. Keith was quickly hauled into the office, and had to sit there completely naked until his dad brought him some clothes. Keith learned his lesson through being humbled. To my knowledge, he never streaked again.

Two Sides of Pride

It is amazing what pride can do to a person. It is just like peer pressure—it has two effects. First, it can be positive, enabling a person to boldly take a stand for what he or she believes. Take dating, for instance. Jeanette told Bob to "go soak his head" when he kept asking her to become sexually involved with him. It was Jeanette's pride that allowed her to be bold, no matter what Bob (or any other Bozo) thought.

Secondly, pride can also be a negative. To refuse the Lord liberty in our lives, and continue to be "hard-headed," is a costly decision. Notice this:

> How much better to get wisdom than gold,
>   to choose understanding rather than silver!
> The highway of the upright avoids evil;
>   he who guards his way guards his life.
> Pride goes before destruction,
>   a haughty spirit before a fall.
> Better to be lowly in spirit and among the
>   oppressed
>   than to share plunder with the proud.
>   (Proverbs 16:16–19)

> Haughty eyes and a proud heart,
>   the lamp of the wicked, are sin! (21:4)

A person who would agree with Scripture about pride tells his story in Daniel 4. Of all people he is King Nebuchadnezzar.

Like Daniel 2, Daniel 4 records that the king had a dream. This time he doesn't waste time with the others to get an interpretation. He goes directly to Daniel. Again, Daniel shows his remarkable character and quality lifestyle. He could easily fit the song "I Need A Hero! He's gotta be strong, and he's gotta be fast, and he's gotta be larger than life."

After telling Daniel the contents of the dream, the king waits for an interpretation. Daniel, though troubled initially, gives the meaning. Imagine being in Daniel's sandals and dropping this "bomb" on "His Majesty":

> This is the interpretation, O king, and this is the decree the Most High has issued against my lord the king: You will be driven away from people and will live with the wild animals; you will eat grass like cattle and be drenched with the dew of heaven. Seven times will pass by for you until you acknowledge that the Most High is sovereign over the kingdoms of men and gives them to anyone he wishes. The command to leave the stump of the tree with its roots means that your kingdom will be restored to you when you acknowledge that Heaven rules. Therefore, O king, be pleased to accept my advice: Renounce your sins by doing what is right, and your wickedness by being kind to the oppressed. It may be that then your prosperity will continue. (4:24–27)

Unbelievable! Daniel could have very easily been

killed for even speaking so bluntly to the irrational King Nebuchadnezzar. No doubt, Daniel recalled the "temper tantrums" the king often had. Yet, Daniel, with courage and honesty, tells the king the truth. Nebuchadnezzar is either to surrender his wicked pride, or eat "humble pie."

That's why Daniel is a hero. Being a hero goes beyond walking around smelling good all the time. A hero is in the trenches, sweating it out with the rest of the team. A hero models courage to live by. And Daniel is a hero because he stayed on the cutting edge, even when it wasn't easy or fun. What a difference!

Some time ago I heard Chuck Swindoll make a statement that I haven't been able to shake off: "It's possible to be too big to be used by God; it's impossible to be too small to be used by God." That's powerful! Marie proved it one day in her class. I used Marie as an illustration of courage in the book, *Here's a Hero: Joseph.* Her bravery deserves to be highlighted again:

> A real hero is someone from whom we can draw strength, courage and inspiration. His or her life is an example that points us to the Hero of heroes, Jesus Christ.
>
> Marie is such a person. She lives in Quito, Ecuador. During spring break one year, our singing group at Toccoa Falls College traveled to Ecuador to give several concerts. They sang in public schools, churches and marketplaces throughout Quito, sharing the love of Jesus.

Following a concert at a high school, one teacher was making fun of the group, saying the members of the group were stupid for believing in Jesus Christ. She said the only thing that was true was humanism and living for yourself. Finally, one person had enough of the teacher's comments.

Marie stood up and spoke out for Jesus. She said she was a Christian and loved God with all her heart. If the teacher would read the Bible, she too would come to love God. When the class saw 95-pound Marie make this stand, other Christian students also began speaking out. As the discussion continued, many non-Christian teens asked questions about Jesus.

When the bell rang at the end of the period, Marie received a standing ovation. Because she was not willing to let the teacher openly mock Jesus, Marie became a hero to her class.[1]

Right on, Marie! Though small, she exercised her pride in her Lord. God uses people, no matter what size. The thing that stops Him is pride. The proof is in Daniel 4 in the life of the king.

All this happened to King Nebuchadnezzar. Twelve months later, as the king was walking on the roof of the royal palace of Babylon, he said, "Is not this the great Babylon I have built as the royal residence, by my mighty power and for the glory of my majesty?"

The words were still on his lips when a voice

came from heaven, "This is what is decreed for you, King Nebuchadnezzar: Your royal authority has been taken from you. You will be driven away from people and will live with the wild animals; you will eat grass like cattle. Seven times will pass by for you until you acknowledge that the Most High is sovereign over the kingdoms of men and gives them to anyone he wishes."

Immediately what had been said about Nebuchadnezzar was fulfilled. He was driven away from people and ate grass like cattle. His body was drenched with the dew of heaven until his hair grew like the feathers of an eagle and his nails like the claws of a bird. (4:28–33)

Do you question how serious God is about pride? Remember this happened to Nebuchadnezzar, the most powerful man on the face of the earth. Yet Daniel, who walked with a passion for God, was successful. The difference: he had a humble heart before God.

Maybe you are thinking, "That only happened in the Bible days." Guess again! Billy Graham reminds us God can humble any "bighead." Listen to this!

I recently heard the story of a mother in an African nation who came to Christ, and grew strong in her commitment and devotion to the Lord. As so often happens, however, this alienated her from her husband, and over the years he grew to despise and hate her new devotion to Christ.

His anger and bitterness reached their climax when he decided to kill his wife, their two children and himself, unable to live in such self-inflicted misery. But he needed a motive. He decided that he would accuse her of stealing his precious keys—the keys were to the bank, the house and the car. Early one afternoon he left his bank and headed for the tavern. His route took him across a footbridge extended over the headwaters of the Nile River. He paused above the river and dropped the keys. He spent all afternoon drinking and carousing.

Later that afternoon, his wife went to the fish market to buy the evening meal. She purchased a large Nile perch. *As she was gutting the fish, in its belly were her husband's keys.* How had they gotten there? What were the circumstances? She did not know; but she cleaned them up and hung them on the hook.

Sufficiently drunk, the young banker came home that night and pounded open the front door shouting, "Woman, where are my keys?" Already in bed, she got up, picked them off the hook in the bedroom, and handed them to her husband. When he saw the keys, by his own testimony he immediately became sober and was instantly converted. He fell on his knees sobbing, asked for forgiveness, and confessed Jesus Christ as his Lord and Savior.[2]

While the African man had sense enough to

repent, the king in all his pride and selfishness did not. For seven years, he was an insane, wild, fearful person. However, he did not stay that way. God restored him, and made him mightier than before. Notice the words of the king himself:

At the end of that time, I, Nebuchadnezzar, raised my eyes toward heaven, and my sanity was restored. Then I praised the Most High; I honored and glorified him who lives forever.

His dominion is an eternal dominion;
  his kingdom endures from generation to
    generation.
All the peoples of the earth
  are regarded as nothing.
He does as he pleases
  with the powers of heaven
  and the peoples of the earth.
No one can hold back his hand
  or say to him: "What have you done?"

At the same time that my sanity was restored, my honor and splendor were returned to me for the glory of my kingdom. My advisers and nobles sought me out, and I was restored to my throne and became even greater than before. Now I, Nebuchadnezzar, praise and exalt and glorify the King of heaven, because everything he does is right and all his ways are just. And those who walk in pride he is able to humble. (4:34–37)

Daniel—what a model of integrity. His relationship with the Lord allowed him to know God's heart and even share with the most ungodly what God was saying. This young man was used of God because his pride was only in the fact that he walked with the Lord consistently. What a difference!

How does a teen do that? How did the king come to acknowledge the uniqueness of Daniel over others? Because God liked him better than others? Did he take a special course in school? Did he have natural abilities, like some people who can play a piano without ever taking lessons? What is the secret?

God does give people at various times in life an extra measure of grace. God also gives people extraordinary abilities because of their passion to walk only God's way.

Daniel had that kind of passion. He was determined to be God's man exclusively. Unfortunately, Nebuchadnezzar had a passion for pride, and he paid the price. A passion for the Lord is like the passion a pro football player has to win. Without this drive, the opponent will have the higher score every time. The opponent to be defeated is pride. Listen to this conversation as it relates to the passion of walking with God.

> He was the first professional athlete I had ever known personally. And in his prime as a football player he was an all-pro pass defender, the best in his business. Like many people I was drawn to him, to the force within him that made him a

winner, a man with the courage to put his body on the line against an opponent before 75,000 people.

On a Monday, six days before his team would play the Dallas Cowboys, the two of us were having lunch together. The upcoming game was the subject of our conversation. "How will you prepare yourself for the Cowboy pass offense?" I asked him. "What will your schedule be this week?"

"Well the mornings will be a practice at the stadium," he answered. "And then I'll go home to my den and load the projector (these were the days before VCRs) with game films, and I'll study the Cowboy receivers until I know all of them better than their wives do. I'll check every movement they make when they come out of the huddles to see if they reveal what sort of play it's going to be, what pattern they're going to run, or whether or not they are going to stay back and block."

"What about your evenings?" I asked.

"Oh I'll keep watching those films straight through until midnight every night."

"Ten hours a day? All week? Nothing else?" I was incredulous.

"Easily," he responded. "Hey, I want to beat those men. I want to hit them so hard if they come into my zone that when they're lying on the ground, they'll look up to the sky with glassy eyes and pray that there won't have to be another play in the game. I want to totally

dominate their spirits."
That's passion speaking! Extreme, powerful passion![3]

That kind of passion, when dedicated to the Lord, is what will divide the Daniels from the "ding-a-lings." A passionate desire to win over the patterns of selfish pride separates the winners from the quitters. All else is pounded into the ground in the contest against arrogance.

Is God speaking to you about being arrogant? If so, come clean before the Lord and be released from the bondage of pride. Ask for a change today. One teen had that kind of relationship with God. Result: Daniel set the pace for the rest of us to follow.

As I said before, anyone can do drugs, booze it up and party their brains out. No special skills needed for that. The same is true for mediocre Christianity. No special qualities are needed to sit in church writing notes and goof off at youth meetings. Any hammerhead can disrupt a Sunday School class or mouth off to the teacher. Even a four-year-old can do that without special training.

Why not be different? Ask God to make you passionate to excel in His way. See if the Lord will choose you to be a hero. God is looking for someone with guts.

Sure beats sitting in the dean's office naked, or eating grass like cattle or having your wife find your keys after a fishing trip!

Putting It into My Life

1. Have you ever been humbled? Was it really em-

barrassing? What was the hardest part of the experience? How did you cope? Have you learned to laugh about it yet? What do you think the Lord was trying to say to you through that time?

2. Describe the two sides to pride. Have you seen any of it in "action"? What was the worst part? The best? Did you learn anything by it? What?

3. How do you think Daniel had the courage to say to the king what he did about his future? Do you think he was nervous at all? Why?

4. Is it possible for teens to have courage like Marie did to stand up for the Lord in her classroom? How can that be something anybody can have? Do you have that kind of courage? Would you like to?

5. React to the last sentence in Daniel 4. "And those who walk in pride he is able to humble." Is that a threat or a warning? Do you think God is serious about this? Why?

6. What did you think of the pro football player who said he wanted to know opponents better than their wives? Is it possible to have a strategy to win over evil pride like the football player wanted to win over the opposing team? Describe that kind of passion. Have you got it?

7

The Cost of
Confrontation

It is amazing how some people react when confronted. Some lie, turn red, shake, or even stutter as they try to respond or defend themselves. Others cry. Then there are those who say nothing. That is hard, because you never know if they are feeling guilty, thinking about killing themselves (or you), or wondering how soon the next batch of Big Macs will be ready at McDonalds.

I have never met a person yet who enjoyed being confronted. Most people I know wiggle and squirm when addressed about a negative issue. No one wakes up saying: "I sure hope I get caught doing something wrong today. That would be just great!"

Sometimes confrontations can be comical. One I saw in the eighth grade was hilarious. Juan was a Spanish-speaking kid in our class. One day the teacher thought she saw him cheating on a test. When confronted, he acted like he didn't understand English well enough to respond to the accusations. It was like an instant case of amnesia. She said, "Do you like to cheat, Juan?" He responded, "Sí, I like chicken." The class roared with laughter, totally frustrating the teacher to where she gave up. Juan sat smiling, looking like the cat that ate the canary. It was amazing, however, how he recovered his English speaking skills when he wanted to impress Jill in the cafeteria.

The worst response, however, is when people try to manipulate their way out of a high pressured situation. When confronted, they find the "escape hatch" and make you look like the stupid jerk all along. Have you ever had that happen? Makes you want to take somebody by the tongue and pull them inside out, doesn't it?

Christian psychologist Dr. James Dobson tells of a little boy who was famous for being a manipulator. Little Robert was the terror of the neighborhood. No one could control him, and when confronted by his mother, he always threatened to do something worse if she didn't leave him alone. However, "Bobby-boy" met his match one day. Listen as Dr. Dobson tells this hilarious story:

> In the absence of parental leadership, some children become extremely obnoxious and defiant, especially in public places. Perhaps the best example was a ten-year-old boy named Robert, who was a patient of my good friend Dr.

William Slonecker. Dr. Slonecker said his pediatric staff dreaded the days when Robert was scheduled for an office visit. He literally attacked the clinic, grabbing instruments and files and telephones. His passive mother could do little more than shake her head in bewilderment.

During one physical examination, Dr. Slonecker observed severe cavities in Robert's teeth and knew that the boy must be referred to a local dentist. But who would be given the honor? A referral like Robert could mean the end of a professional friendship. Dr. Slonecker eventually decided to send him to an older dentist who reportedly understood children. The confrontation that followed now stands as one of the classic moments in the history of human conflict.

Robert arrived in the dental office, prepared for battle.

"Get in the chair, young man," said the doctor.

"No chance!" replied the boy.

"Son, I told you to climb onto the chair, and that's what I intend for you to do," said the dentist.

"If you make me get in that chair, I will take off all my clothes."

The dentist calmly said, "Son, take 'em off."

The boy forthwith removed his shirt, undershirt, shoes and socks, and then looked up in defiance.

"All right, son," said the dentist. "Now get on the chair."

"You didn't hear me," sputtered Robert. "I said

if you make me get on that chair, I will take off all my clothes."

"Son, take 'em off," replied the man.

Robert proceeded to remove his pants and shorts, finally standing totally naked before the dentist and his assistant.

"Now, son, get in the chair," said the doctor.

Robert did as he was told, and sat cooperatively through the entire procedure. When the cavities were drilled and filled, he was instructed to step down from the chair.

"Give me my clothes now," said the boy.

"I'm sorry," replied the dentist. "Tell your mother that we're going to keep your clothes tonight. She can pick them up tomorrow."

Can you comprehend the shock Robert's mother received when the door to the waiting room opened and there stood her pink son, as naked as the day he was born? The room was filled with patients, but Robert and his mom walked past them into the hall. They went down a public elevator and into the parking lot, ignoring the snickers of onlookers.

The next day, Robert's mother returned to retrieve his clothes, and asked to have a word with the dentist. However, she did not come to protest. These were her sentiments: "You don't know how much I appreciate what happened here yesterday. You see, Robert has been blackmailing me about his clothes for years. Whenever we are in a public place, such as a grocery store, he makes unreasonable demands of me. If

I don't immediately buy him what he wants, he threatens to take off all his clothes. You are the first person who has called his bluff, doctor, and the impact on Robert has been incredible."[1]

Just as the dentist was great at addressing a kid who needed to "meet his match," God also is aware of how to get our attention. The Lord has grace and compassion, but there are limits. Daniel 5 records a night in history when a king named Belshazzar overstepped those boundaries.

At this point in history King Nebuchadnezzar has died, and been replaced by Belshazzar. He had no regard for the things of the Lord, and dismissed the final message King Nebuchadnezzar gave to Babylon about God being able to humble the proud. Belshazzar was like my friend Juan—he pretended he didn't understand. Yet he was soon to learn a new language.

King Belshazzar gave a great banquet for a thousand of his nobles and drank wine with them. While Belshazzar was drinking his wine, he gave orders to bring in the gold and silver goblets that Nebuchadnezzar his father had taken from the temple in Jerusalem, so that the king and his nobles, his wives and his concubines might drink from them. So they brought in the gold goblets that had been taken from the temple of God in Jerusalem, and the king and his nobles, his wives and his concubines drank from them. As they drank the wine, they praised the gods of gold and silver, of bronze, iron, wood and stone.

Suddenly the fingers of a human hand appeared and wrote on the plaster of the wall, near the lampstand in the royal palace. The king watched the hand as it wrote. His face turned pale and he was so frightened that his knees knocked together and his legs gave way. (5:1–6)

The wicked king had the courage to defy God by using the gold and silver goblets from the temple as "party accessories." But as the hand and fingers of a man appeared and began to write on the wall, suddenly the party was over. God had come, not to celebrate, but to pull the plug on the band, shut out the lights and pronounce the benediction. He had come to confront eyeball to eyeball.

Like the previous king, King Belshazzar called in some astrologers to interpret for him what the writing meant. They could not figure it out. As the king begins to get "green around the gills," his wife appears and tells the king about Daniel, one who can "interpret dreams, explain riddles and solve difficult problems" (5:12). Immediately, Daniel is called for. At this point, the king is willing to do anything, even listen to a godly man. Our hero responds true to his character:

So Daniel was brought before the king, and the king said to him, "Are you Daniel, one of the exiles my father the king brought from Judah? I have heard that the spirit of the gods is in you

93

and that you have insight, intelligence and out-standing wisdom. The wise men and enchanters were brought before me to read this writing and tell me what it means, but they could not explain it. Now I have heard that you are able to give interpretations and to solve difficult problems. If you can read this writing and tell me what it means, you will be clothed in purple and have a gold chain placed around your neck, and you will be made the third highest ruler in the kingdom."

Then Daniel answered the king, "You may keep your gifts for yourself and give your rewards to someone else. Nevertheless, I will read the writing for the king and tell him what it means." (5:13–17)

What a quality person Daniel is. With the same courage needed to speak to King Nebuchadnezzar, he addresses this king. Although Belshazzar was Nebuchadnezzar's son, Daniel approaches the monarch with the same dignity and confidence in the Lord. He, a slave, stands with shoulders squared and confronts the king with what God gave him that night.

O King, the Most High God gave your father Nebuchadnezzar sovereignty and greatness and glory and splendor.

But you his son, O Belshazzar, have not humbled yourself, though you knew all this. Instead, you have set yourself up against the Lord of heaven. You had the goblets from his temple brought to you, and you and your nobles, your wives and your concubines drank wine from them. You praised the gods of silver and gold, of bronze, iron, wood and stone, which cannot see or hear or understand. But you did not honor the God who holds in his hand your life and all your ways. Therefore he sent the hand that wrote the inscription.

This is the inscription that was written:

MENE, MENE, TEKEL, PARSIN

This is what these words mean:

Mene: God has numbered the days of your
     reign and brought it to an end.
Tekel: You have been weighed on the scales
     and found wanting.
Peres: Your kingdom is divided and given to
     the Medes and Persians. (5:18, 22–28)

Can you imagine what this world leader must have been thinking when he was confronted by this slave with a message from God? He who had been the epitome of pride is informed that his parade just got rained on permanently.

There are plenty of "Belshazzars" in our world today: "Poison," "Jane's Addiction," "2 Live Crew," "House of Lords," and "The Dead Kennedys" to name a few. Those like Prince, Ozzy Osborne and Madonna, who so blatantly reduce the sacred and holy things of God into a form of foolish superstition, will one day be confronted. Just as Belshazzar grew pale, and became so frightened that his knees knocked, so will those who have laughed at, offended and mocked Almighty God. The satanists in that day will realize their end has come. Those who have considered godliness to be something for children, old maids, and wimps, will suddenly discover who the wimps are—them!—and who the winners are—those who have loved God and given Him their lives forever. Belshazzar was shown the end of his life written on the wall. We also read the end of wickedness as it is written in God's Holy Book.

> From the west, men will fear the name
>   of the LORD,
>   and from the rising of the sun, they will
>   revere his glory.
> For he will come like a pent-up flood
>   that the breath of the LORD drives along.
>   (Isaiah 59:19)

> But with righteousness he will judge the needy,
>   with justice he will give decisions for the poor
>   of the earth.
> He will strike the earth with the rod of his
>   mouth;
>   with the breath of his lips he will slay the
>   wicked. (11:4)

And I tell you that you are Peter, and on this

rock I will build my church, and the gates of Hades will not overcome it. (Matthew 16:18)

God is just: He will pay back trouble to those who trouble you and give relief to you who are troubled, and to us as well. This will happen when the Lord Jesus is revealed from heaven in blazing fire with his powerful angels. (2 Thessalonians 1:6–7)

Then I saw the beast and the kings of the earth and their armies gathered together to make war against the rider on the horse and his army. But the beast was captured, and with him the false prophet who had performed the miraculous signs on his behalf. With these signs he had deluded those who had received the mark of the beast and worshiped his image. The two of them were thrown alive into the fiery lake of burning sulfur. (Revelation 19:19–20)

It's true—God not only confronts the wicked by writing on the wall, but He also writes it in history, and in His word.

Understanding the Concept of Confrontation

To make sure we realize how confrontation is to be understood, let's crystallize the main ideas:

1. God may appear as slow as cold honey, but He is always complete. Rest in this: God is never late. It is His compassion that holds the process of destruc-

tion. However, when confrontation against evil arises, it will be swift.

> For if God did not spare angels when they sinned, but sent them to hell, putting them into gloomy dungeons to be held for judgment; if he did not spare the ancient world when he brought the flood on its ungodly people, but protected Noah, a preacher of righteousness, and seven others; if he condemned the cities of Sodom and Gomorrah by burning them to ashes, and made them an example of what is going to happen to the ungodly; and if he rescued Lot, a righteous man, who was distressed by the filthy lives of lawless men . . . if this is so, then the Lord knows how to rescue godly men from trials and to hold the unrighteous for the day of judgment, while continuing their punishment. This is especially true of those who follow the corrupt desire of the sinful nature and despise authority. (2 Peter 2:4–7, 9–10a)

2. Honoring the Lord is worth the effort. A godly reputation is worth cherishing. Cultivate and protect the things of God. Because of his convictions, Daniel had the audience of kings. Even Belshazzar rewarded him for his godly faithfulness.

> Then at Belshazzar's command, Daniel was clothed in purple, a gold chain was placed around his neck, and he was proclaimed the third highest ruler in the kingdom. (5:29)

So we will be rewarded for what we have done (Revelation 22:12). As Daniel had the audience of kings, so we have audience with the King of kings—Jesus. By accepting His confrontation against evil for us, our Savior gives us access into the throne room of heaven.

3. God has the last word. Just look at how Daniel 5 concludes:

> That very night Belshazzar, king of the Babylonians, was slain, and Darius the Mede took over the kingdom, at the age of sixty-two. (5:30–31)

Belshazzar's wickedness was accounted for. *That very night* he was killed by an invading king named Darius, who took the throne of Babylon, a direct prediction of Daniel.

Maybe you have been wondering if God is really serious about confrontation. Now that you have seen what happened to the king, are you convinced? If you have been floundering, confront those fears and ask the Lord to give you the confidence he gave to Daniel long ago. He will give you a message to share also. It will be that "the one who is in you is greater than the one who is in the world" (1 John 4:4b).

Go for it!

Putting It into My Life

1. How do you react when you are confronted? Is

there a tendency to lie, manipulate, get angry, lash back or clam up? Why do you react that way?

2. What do you do if you have to confront someone? Is it pleasant? Do you get nervous? Are you afraid of losing their friendship? Are you unsure of their commitment? Do you fear rejection?

3. Do you see what offended God by Belshazzar drinking and partying with the temple utensils? What were the cups for? How were they abused?

4. How do you feel when you read that God will stamp out all evil one day? Glad? Relieved? Confident? Nervous? Why?

5. Respond to the three parts of the concept of confrontation. Do you believe they are true? Are they challenging to you? Why?

6. If God has "the last word," what would He have to confront in your life? Would you listen? Are you wanting to change something now? Will you do it?

8

Consistency—
A Hero's Focus

"A Winner Never Quits—And a Quitter Never Wins." In my mind, I can still see those words on a large poster that hung on the wall in our high school football locker room. Like chants and clapping at a pep rally, those words motivated us to keep trying our best as we tackled, blocked, passed and did routine drills in daily practice. Before a game, they triggered a drive to excel above the competition. Often the coach would close his pep talk with that phrase, causing such an excitement within every player we thought we would explode! Like a drummer in a marching band pounding out a rhythm heard throughout the stadium, those words were pounded into us, affirming that consistency makes the difference between winners and quitters. It is by consistency that:

- a student becomes a doctor
- an average player works and becomes MVP
- an average musician becomes a phenomenal musician, and packs out a concert hall
- an athlete goes to the Olympics
- a former drug abuser stays "clean"
- an abused person refuses to allow bitterness to invade
- a team takes the state or national championship.

Winners win because they refuse to quit. Commitment to consistency makes winners a breed apart. History records how consistency made average people into heroes.

We Can Overcome

Some of the world's greatest men and women have been saddled with disabilities and adversities but have managed to overcome them.

Cripple him, and you have Sir Walter Scott.

Lock him in a prison cell, and you have John Bunyan.

Bury him in the snows of Valley Forge, and you have a George Washington.

Raise him in abject poverty, and you have an Abraham Lincoln.

Subject him to bitter religious prejudice, and you have a Disraeli.

Strike him down with infantile paralysis, and he becomes a Franklin D. Roosevelt.

Burn him so severely in a schoolhouse fire that

the doctors say he will never walk again, and you have a Glenn Cunningham, who set the world's record in 1934 for running a mile in 4 minutes and 6.7 seconds.

Deafen a genius composer, and you have a Ludwig van Beethoven.

Have him or her born black in a society filled with racial discrimination, and you have a Booker T. Washington, a Harriet Tubman, a Marian Anderson, a George Washington Carver, or a Martin Luther King, Jr.

Make him the first child to survive in a poor Italian family of eighteen children, and you have an Enrico Caruso.

Have him born of parents who survived a Nazi concentration camp, paralyze him from the waist down when he is four, and you have an incomparable concert violinist, Itzhak Perlman.

Call him a slow learner, "retarded," and write him off as uneducable, and you have an Albert Einstein.[1]

Without consistency and determination when life seemed to be consistantly difficult, any one of those people would have just been another face or number. By their perseverance they became winners!

Do you see the common thread of consistency woven in the fabric of these people? When no one was around to clap, play their music, pat their back or write about them in a book, they were consistent.

Meeting people like those listed above is thrilling. It is as though they have a contagious spirit about them. They offer hope in desperate situations, and seem to say to all who hear about them, "If I can make it, anyone can make it." My mom demonstrates that to many people. She has served the Lord since she was a teenager, and though she has had difficult points in her life, she has always remained true. Her consistency is the hallmark of a quality relationship that doesn't get washed out with the first little storm that blows.

In Daniel 6, we find another model of consistency. Although a slave, removed from his family in his teen years, and subjected to abuse and neglect, Daniel remained true to God's way. When his convictions were ridiculed, he followed the Lord anyway. Though his friends nearly became "french fries" in Nebuchadnezzar's furnace, Daniel was unbending in his commitment to godliness. When he could have been killed for speaking negatively in the presence of the king, once again, Daniel was faithful in his stand. Not once is there a hint of complaining or bitterness in his life. Consistency makes Daniel a hero.

> It pleased Darius to appoint 120 satraps to rule throughout the kingdom, with three administrators over them, one of whom was Daniel. The satraps were made accountable to them so that the king might not suffer loss. Now Daniel so distinguished himself among the administrators and the satraps by his exceptional qualities that the king planned to set him over the whole kingdom. At this, the administrators

and the satraps tried to find grounds for charges against Daniel in his conduct of government affairs, but they were unable to do so. They could find no corruption in him, because he was trustworthy and neither corrupt nor negligent. (6:1–4)

Did you see the character quality being shown? Genuineness, seen in key phrases like "distinguished himself," "his exceptional qualities," "no corruption in him," "was trustworthy," "neither corrupt nor negligent," seems to shout: "THIS GUY IS FOR REAL! BE LIKE HIM."

Rewriting the Rules

Daniel—what a role model! In a day when cheating seems to be one's only chance to excel, and being a leader often means being a liar, Daniel steps in and rewrites the script. His lifestyle is true and honest. He yanks the idea of cheating and lying right out of the "How to Win with Deception" textbook, and heaves it in the nearest dumpster. His example gives us courage to take the deception of our times, wad it up, and bag it with the rest of the trash. It's time for some teens to follow the example of Daniel! Are you willing to "rewrite the rules" in your school, on your team, and in your neighborhood? Instead of the violence, drugs, cheating and hatred, why not take the challenge to set the example of honesty, love and trustworthiness?

It is always inspiring to find people who won over the odds. Their stories make us want to run, swim, box, repair, work, dive, practice, sweat—whatever, to be like them. Their zeal gives us an energy and pattern to follow. Yet, it cannot stop there. If we lose the enthusiasm, and the bright examples of others begin to fade, then what? How can a person stay focused on their intentions?

Focus on Consistency

Along with inspiring stories, we need to grasp how to remain consistent ourselves! Daniel gives us those principles of consistency. Let's highlight them and then find ways to put them into everyday living.

1. *Daniel Had a Terrific Attitude.* Daniel 6:3 says he "so distinguished himself . . ." This does not mean he was arrogant, "stuck-up" or conceited, but he was determined to be the best he could be. That difference was developed by keeping a good attitude. What a great quality to find.

Steve was like that. He was always positive to be with. Working with him at car washes and on lawn jobs was great because he was a positive person. His personality affected those he was with, no matter if he was playing ball, doing a group report, or working on a project.

Jim was just the opposite. His attitude was negative and he always had a whine in his tone. He walked around with a face so long he could have sucked marbles out of a gopher hole. His attitude was so sour, he looked like he had just been baptized in lemon juice.

How do people get to be positive or negative in

their attitudes? One word: *choice*. Daniel had a choice. He could have been negative. Who would have blamed him for being negative as a slave? But he chose to do the opposite. Daniel chose to have a terrific attitude. Excellent!

What do you do to evaluate your attitude? In *Here's a Hero: Joseph*, I give guidelines for consistency I have found that work. See what you think:

• Do I honor everyone in authority over me—my parents, teachers, coaches, youth leaders and others?

• Am I on time for class and with assignments, or do I have a tendency to be late? Do I do what my parents ask me to do when they ask me to do it? Or do I do the things when it suits me to do them?

• Do I meet the responsibilities given to me? Do my parents, teachers or youth leaders think of me when extra work is needed?

• Do I look for ways of improving my performance, or am I content to carry on as usual?

• If I was evaluated by those I am responsible to, what would they say? Improve? Doing great? Weak?[2]

It is a choice to have a good attitude. Have you decided to do that, or did you fall into the lemon juice too?

2. *Daniel Was Faithful in His Work.* Being faithful is being consistent: It is a continual process, even when others rationalize, get lazy, lie, or wiggle their

way out of responsibility. The price is high, but being on the cutting edge requires paying the dues. Daniel did and became a winner. Winners have no regrets about paying the high price of faithfulness in order to achieve, while quitters shop around for a better bargain. To be above the average doesn't come cheap. Wendy Stoker, a teen from Iowa, would agree. Without her perseverance, she would still be waiting for "the good deal."

Born in Cedar Rapids, Iowa, Wendy became interested in watersports. In high school she placed third, just 2 1/2 points from first place in the Iowa girl's state diving championship. She worked two hours a day for four years to be at such a high competitive level. Listen to the rest of her story:

> Now at the University of Florida, she's working twice as hard and has earned the number two position on the varsity diving team, and she's aiming for the national finals. Wendy is carrying a full academic load, finds time for bowling and is an accomplished water-skier.
>
> But perhaps the most remarkable thing about Wendy Stoker is her typing. She bangs out forty five words a minute on her typewriter—with her toes.
>
> Oh, did I fail to mention? Wendy was born without arms.[3]

That is faithfulness. It isn't cheap, but it is what separates the winners from the quitters. It appears in Daniel's life over and over. He practiced faithfulness in his life like Wendy practiced diving—until he was a champion.

3. *His Strength Was in His Relationship with the Lord.* Notice Daniel 6:5; "Finally these men said, 'We will never find any basis for charges against this man Daniel unless it has something to do with the law of his God.'" Daniel's public life had the qualities of a hero because his personal life was secure in the Lord. Daniel had one passion—to honor the Lord. No wonder he was such an outstanding person—he honored the Lord. God tells us if we will honor Him, He will honor us.

> Therefore the LORD, the God of Israel, declares: "I promised that your house and your father's house would minister before me forever." But now the LORD declares: "Far be it from me! Those who honor me I will honor, but those who despise me will be disdained." (1 Samuel 2:30b)

> Trust in the LORD with all your heart
>   and lean not on your own understanding;
> in all your ways acknowledge him,
>   and he will make your paths straight.
>   (Proverbs 3:5–6)

> Humble yourselves, therefore, under God's mighty hand, that he may lift you up in due time. Cast all your anxiety on him because he cares for you. (1 Peter 5:6–7)

Come to me, all you who are weary and burdened, and I will give you rest. Take my yoke upon you and learn from me, for I am gentle and humble in heart, and you will find rest for your souls. For my yoke is easy and my burden is light. (Matthew 11:28–30)

When people apply the Scriptures to their life, their relationship with the Lord is serious. Changes come. Time spent in discovering God's principles and then applying them to life develops a special quality within people. This is not to be confused with a "warm and fuzzy" feeling. Anybody can work that up. It even goes beyond the "crisis-oriented" relationships some people have. We've all seen those who, when in trouble, decide to "be more religious."

- Jenny prayed to God when she found out she was failing geometry.
- Fearing his father, Sam asked God for help when he got caught shoplifting.
- Douglas suddenly felt he should pray when he wrecked his brother-in-law's Corvette while driving to his girlfriend's house without permission.
- When Cindy's doctor confirmed that her pregnancy test was positive, she wondered if God would hear her if she prayed.

These are all "crisis-oriented." When a crisis arrives, suddenly they are oriented toward God. But it is always disappointing to see people not go on in this relationship. They start out potential winners, but end up quitting. What a drag!

Not so with Daniel. He was consistent in having a terrific attitude, and in being faithful in every area of his life. Result: he could also be consistent in finding that his strength was in his daily relationship with God. There's the difference between a warrior and a wimp, between a winner and a quitter.

Being consistent made Daniel outstanding. That consistency was throughout his total person because of one word: Choice. He *chose* to have an outstanding attitude. He *chose* to be faithful in every area of his life. He *chose* to serve the Lord every day. As a result, he had a quality about him that divides the winners from the quitters.

Making these choices is not always easy. There are times when it would be more convenient to be like everyone else—wear the same clothes, tell the same jokes, do the same things, date the same way, cheat on the same exams, tell the same lies and fail to be anything but the same failure. But wouldn't it be more worthwhile to make your life count for something? To be different? To have a standard and quality about you that would inspire people to be better than the average?

It's true: there is a price to pay. However, failure isn't cheap in the end. Just listen to these challenges, and dare to be different as you dare to choose consistency, faithfulness and spending time with the Lord every day:

There is a certain blend of courage . . . character, and principle which has no satisfactory dictionary name, but has been called different things at different times in different countries. Our American name for it is "guts."[4]

Putting It into My Life

1. "A Winner Never Quits and A Quitter Never Wins." When have you seen that principle work? In whom? How? Can you apply that to your life today? How?

2. Define consistency. How does it connect to determination? Faithfulness? Who is the most consistent person you know? How? Can you implement their example to help you in your relationship with the Lord?

3. What are some ways Daniel was consistent? Do you think it was easy? In your opinion, what would have been the hardest time for Daniel to remain consistent to the Lord? Why?

4. Do you see lying and cheating in leaders today? What is your reaction? Do you think you could be as Daniel was when he saw it in his day? How can you take the challenge to be different as he was?

9

Standing Up to Attacks

Chuck Swindoll relates this story of a life-and-death struggle:

Several years ago I read a true story about a man who was hunting deer. As he climbed to a ledge and raised his head to look over the edge, a coiled rattlesnake struck with lightning speed, just missing his ear. The fangs of the four-foot snake got snagged in the neck of the hunter's turtleneck sweater, and the force of its strike landed the reptile on his shoulder. It then coiled around his neck. Thankfully, the man had enough presence of mind to grab the snake behind the head when he felt its warm venom running down his skin.

Suddenly, the man lost his footing, fell backward, and slid headfirst down the steep rocky slope, ending up wedged between two boulders. Struggling to disengage the fangs from his sweater, he unwittingly freed the creature enough to provide it the leverage to strike again and again . . . about eight times in all. Miraculously, each strike missed by a hair. The ugly fangs looked like giant needles, frightening up close. Finally, at the point of exhaustion, the man was somehow able to choke the snake to death. When he tried to toss the limp creature aside, however, he couldn't let go of it without literally prying his fingers from its neck.[1]

After reading that incredible account, I was reminded how closely the hunter's experience is like a life dedicated to honesty, courage and dignity. Just when it looks as though the top of a mountain in life is reached, a surprise attack comes attempting to inject poison into a person. The goal of the surprise is to cause the downfall of the hero.

When those attacks strike, it is with the intention to kill. I have never read of a hero who, while climbing to their maximum potential, didn't have someone try to cut their support ropes, roll boulders at them from the top, or attempt to sink venomous fangs of failure into them. Daniel is no exception.

It pleased Darius to appoint 120 satraps to rule throughout the kingdom, with three administrators over them, one of whom was Daniel. The satraps were made accountable to them so that the king might not suffer loss. Now Daniel so distinguished himself among the administrators and the satraps by his exceptional qualities that the king planned to set him over the whole kingdom. At this, the administrators and the satraps tried to find grounds for charges against Daniel in his conduct of government affairs . . . (Daniel 6:1–4a)

When attacks like this happen, two options are available:

1. You can respond, "That's it! I'm through. You can take this 'leadership/hero/being distinct' stuff and blow it out your ear! I'm tired of the work, the fight and all the other junk that comes with it. Goodbye, leadership, hello easy life."
2. You can do as Daniel did, and stick with your commitment, even when attempts for the jugular vein continue. Verse 4 concludes that, though they tried to find some fault in Daniel, "they were unable to do so. They could find no corruption in him because he was trustworthy and neither corrupt nor negligent."

Standing up to personal criticism can be exasperating. But who ever said climbing the mountains with heroes was a walk in the park?

When Things Get Worse

Finally these men said, "We will never find any

basis for charges against this man Daniel unless it has something to do with the law of his God."

So the administrators and the satraps went as a group to the king and said: "O King Darius, live forever! The royal administrators, prefects, satraps, advisers and governors have all agreed that the king should issue an edict and enforce the decree that anyone who prays to any god or man during the next thirty days, except to you, O king, shall be thrown into the lions' den. Now, O king, issue the decree and put it in writing so that it cannot be altered—in accordance with the laws of the Medes and Persians, which cannot be repealed." So King Darius put the decree in writing. (6:5–9)

Daniel is being set up in a trap not for doing wrong, but for doing right! All his life he had been a person of integrity. Now some are trying to cut his support ropes, and roll boulders at him. Just as the snake was coiled and waiting on top of the rock the hunter climbed, so Daniel is struck at by the snakes who wrote the decree. They want to sink their fangs into his future. What poison!

What would you do? Give up? Join the others? Be a quitter? Hiss back? Be a winner?

I am glad that Daniel didn't quit doing right and stayed true to the Lord. Here's the proof:

Now when Daniel learned that the decree had been published, he went home to his upstairs room where the windows opened toward

Jerusalem. Three times a day he got down on his knees and prayed, giving thanks to his God, just as he had done before. Then these men went as a group and found Daniel praying and asking God for help. So they went to the king and spoke to him about his royal decree: "Did you not publish a decree that during the next thirty days anyone who prays to any god or man except to you, O king, would be thrown into the lions' den?"

The king answered, "The decree stands—in accordance with the laws of the Medes and Persians, which cannot be repealed."

Then they said to the king, "Daniel, who is one of the exiles from Judah, pays no attention to you, O king, or to the decree you put in writing. He still prays three times a day." (6:10–13)

Did you get that? Despite decrees and declarations by a few wimps, Daniel still stands in dignity. Even when it isn't easy, Daniel keeps walking with the Lord. His faithfulness is foremost.

It is amazing how one life can change a situation. One life represents one vote for either good or bad. The choice is made according to what is most valuable to that person. History proves one life and one vote can bring big changes.

- In 1776, one vote gave America the English language instead of German.
- In 1845, one vote brought Texas into the Union.
- In 1868, one vote saved President Andrew Johnson from impeachment.

- In 1876, one vote gave Rutherford B. Hayes the U.S. Presidency.
- In 1923, one vote gave Adolph Hitler control of the Nazi Party.[2]

It's really true that one person can make a difference if he or she commits to a goal. Some examples include:

- 18-year-old Michael Chang, who defeated veteran champion Ivan Lendl in tennis. Despite near-crippling leg cramps, Chang persisted, winning the title. His solid Christian testimony that aired on all the major networks after the victory was equally powerful.
- the Chinese student who, in August of 1989, stood in front of a tank protesting communism in his country. As the world held its breath, all were inspired by his bravery. Who wasn't challenged to take the risks worthy of that most precious gift, freedom?
- the rescuers of 18-month-old Jessica McClure, who was stuck in a well in Midland, Texas for nearly 60 hours. Pounding through several feet of solid rock, laboring day and night to exhaustion, workers were eventually able to bring her out of the narrow passage. Though six operations, an amputation of a little toe and a hospital stay were required, Jessica is now enjoying a normal life thanks to the efforts of those heroes in Midland, Texas.
- Greg Lemond, who won the Tour de France by .08

seconds. This comeback ride came after a severe accident that nearly removed him from racing forever.

- those involved in the rescue effort following the earthquake that hit the San Francisco/Oakland area in October, 1989. Many people risked their lives to save hundreds trapped beneath sections of highway, collapsed buildings and piles of rubble. The tragedy would have escalated had it not been for medical teams, rescue squads, and others trained to be of assistance to the injured and wounded.

- U.S. troops, who rescued the country of Kuwait from its occupation by Iraq. The American soldiers are heroes to those in Kuwait. Had those G.I.'s not come, hopelessness is all that Kuwait would know today.

These stories leave our hearts racing, and our courage climbing. The heroes of these events are significant because of their bravery.

Notice what God says about one person:

For the eyes of the LORD range throughout the earth to strengthen those whose hearts are fully committed to him. (2 Chronicles 16:9a)

"I looked for a man among them who would build the wall and stand before me in the gap on behalf of the land so I would not have to destroy it, but I found none." (Ezekiel 22:30)

They forgot the God who saved them,
 who had done great things in Egypt,
miracles in the land of Ham
 and awesome deeds by the Red Sea.
So he said he would destroy them—
 had not Moses, his chosen one,
stood in the breach before him
 to keep his wrath from destroying them.
  (Psalm 106:21–23)

Without a doubt, Daniel is known more for being thrown into the lions' den than for any other event in his life. Though the story is familiar, watch how our man continues to be a hero worth modeling. If you haven't been impressed with Daniel so far, hold on to your ticket. This guy is about to tame some lions without a chair and whip. Look at this:

> Then they said to the king, "Daniel, who is one of the exiles from Judah, pays no attention to you, O king, or to the decree you put in writing. He still prays three times a day." When the king heard this, he was greatly distressed; he was determined to rescue Daniel and made every effort until sundown to save him.
>
> Then the men went as a group to the king and said to him, "Remember, O king, that according to the law of the Medes and Persians no decree or edict that the king issues can be changed."
>
> So the king gave the order, and they brought Daniel and threw him into the lions' den. The king said to Daniel, "May your God, whom you

serve continually, rescue you!" (Daniel 6:13–16)

When Daniel heard the sound of that stone rolling across that opening, what do you think he had on his mind? As he was lowered into that lions' den, and the gates were pulled up, releasing those 400–500 pound cats from their cages, can you imagine his reaction? How do you think he was praying then?

- God, is this what I get for my devotion to you?
- I thought serving you, Lord, would keep me from all harm.
- Wasn't it enough that I was yanked out of my native country, and forced into this land as a slave?
- How can I trust you now, God?
- I always heard you would be with me. Where are you now God? These lions are roaring as only the king of the beasts can. Can't you hear them, God? Can't you hear me?

Remarkably, Daniel doesn't pray that way at all. In fact, just the opposite is recorded, for he has integrity!

At the first light of dawn, the king got up and hurried to the lions' den. When he came near the den, he called to Daniel in an anguished voice, "Daniel, servant of the living God, has your God, whom you serve continually, been able to rescue you from the lions?"

Daniel answered, "O king, live forever! My

121

God sent his angel, and he shut the mouths of the lions. They have not hurt me, because I was found innocent in his sight. Nor have I ever done wrong before you, O king."

The king was overjoyed and gave orders to lift Daniel out of the den. And when Daniel was lifted from the den, no wound was found on him, because he had trusted in his God. (6:19–23)

Unbelievable! Despite the lies, the lions, and the loneliness of being in that den, once again, Daniel stands tall and powerful as only a real hero can. Nothing is mentioned of fear, anger, bitterness or timidity in Daniel as he spent the night in that cold, damp, dark lions' den. Rather we find phrases like:

"servant of the living God" (v. 20).
"God, whom you serve continually" (v. 20).
"rescue you from the lions" (v. 20).
"My God sent his angel" (v. 22).
"he shut the mouths of lions" (v. 22).
"They have not hurt me" (v. 22).
"I was found innocent" (v. 22).
"Nor have I ever done any wrong before you, O king" (v. 22).
"no wound was found on him" (v. 23).
"he had trusted in his God" (v. 23).

If ever there was a "big moment" for Daniel, it was when he was lifted out of that den, a free man. He was honored by God because he elected to honor the Lord's ways with integrity even in a crisis. He passed the test with flying colors. His heart proved to be bent in only one direction—God's!

No matter how people chose to walk, Daniel kept walking with the Lord, the way he always had, without changing his course. Whether or not his bravery and consistency were acknowledged, Daniel stayed true. He knew where he was going, and was willing to pay the price to get there. Daniel dared to be different, not just for any reason, but for the ultimate reason: honoring God. Result: he is a hero!

To those paddling around in mud puddles and shallow waters, Daniel's life is a challenge to get out into the depths of God's power and make a difference. Any wimp can stand on shore playing with a sand bucket, and shooting a water pistol. God calls us to be warriors who rescue those drowning from the impact of liars, deceivers and manipulators. Listen to this challenge:

> Superficiality is the curse of our age. The doctrine of instant satisfaction is a primary spiritual problem. The desperate need today is not for a greater number of intelligent people, or gifted people, but for deep people.[3]

God honors those who will respond to that kind of challenge. Even as Daniel was recognized by the Lord for being faithful, so He will acknowledge you.

Notice what happened to those who lied about the Lord's man, Daniel:

At the king's command, the men who had false-ly accused Daniel were brought in and thrown into the lions' den, along with their wives and children. And before they reached the floor of the den, the lions overpowered them and crushed all their bones. (6:24)

Even as people are impressed by the remarkable feats of athletes, King Darius was impressed with how God took care of Daniel. The Scripture says so. The king sent a message that went to all of the known world:

Then King Darius wrote to all the peoples, na-tions, and men of every language throughout the land:

"May you prosper greatly!

"I issue a decree that in every part of my kingdom people must fear and reverence the God of Daniel.

"For he is the living God
   and he endures forever;
his kingdom will not be destroyed,
   his dominion will never end.
He rescues and he saves;
   he performs signs and wonders
   in the heavens and on the earth.
He has rescued Daniel
   from the power of the lions." (6:25–27)

124

What a moment for Daniel! Though lied about and heaved into the den of lions, he still remained true. His example is still being told wherever the Bible is taught. Evidently, God thinks very highly of those who dare to be different like Daniel.

How about you? Anyone set a trap for you lately, emotionally lowering you into a den? Maybe some "lions of life" are eyeing you, licking their chops. Perhaps you are wondering where God is now.

Don't give up. God hasn't gone anywhere. His angels are dispatched to that den even as they were to Daniel's. Stay true to the One who has been in that same den before you. Like with Daniel, He is forming you to make a difference. Your consistency will encourage, inspire, challenge and speak to others.

Dare to Be a Daniel
Standing by a purpose true,
Heeding God's command,
Honor them the faithful few!
All hail to Daniel's band!

Many mighty men are lost,
Daring not to stand,
Who for God had been a host
By joining Daniel's band!

Many giants, great and tall,
Stalking through the land,
Headlong to the earth would fall
If met by Daniel's band!

Hold the gospel banner high
On to victory grand!
Satan and his host defy
And shout for Daniel's band!

Dare to be a Daniel,
Dare to stand alone;
Dare to have a purpose firm,
Dare to make it known![4]

Putting It into My Life

1. Imagine you are Daniel. How would you respond to those who lied about you? What would you say to them just prior to being lowered into a den of lions?
2. Daniel never mentioned being angry, mad, bitter, or hostile. How do you think he stayed so calm? How is that possible today?
3. Have you been "lowered into a den" lately? Is it dark? Cold? Lonely? Scary? What is going to happen to you if the "lions of life" continue to roar at you? Is God reshaping and molding you? Can He lift you out a hero too?

10

The Window to Tomorrow

A brick mason was seen every day stopping at a window of a building, placing his hands around his eyes, and peering in at a particular picture. Having done this for many weeks, someone asked him about his habit. "I am a brick mason who works, sweats, and gets dirty laying bricks all day long. The bricks I am laying are to the building pictured in the window. As I am working in the hot sun, I keep the picture in my mind of what the finished product will look like. This keeps me from becoming discouraged."

Studying Daniel has given us many windows to peer through, enabling us to see how, brick upon brick, God makes heroes. The portrait of Daniel inspires us who are sweating and grinding away, trying to make a difference in this world. Our strength comes from the Holy Spirit. Daniel's life gives our lives focus.

Daniel's personal life is painted for us in Daniel 1–6. Daniel 7–12 is about future events, giving a blueprint into the future. To have a complete picture, other books of the Bible need to be studied. However, a basic sketch of tomorrow is clearly seen in Daniel 7–12.

A lot of talk today is about predictions of tomorrow. Palm readers are a dime a dozen, and horoscopes appear in nearly every newspaper in America. The New Age movement has likewise produced some so-called "instruments" that claim to enable us to see into the future. With all of the interest about the future, we need to know what is real. That is why Daniel 7–12 is so helpful. Daniel saw much of our tomorrows in his day. Let's look through the window of his prophecy and see what will occur.

Antichrist, Those in Christ, and Christ Himself

In a nutshell, Daniel speaks about the last days of the world in three categories: The Antichrist, those in Christ (or the church), and Christ Himself. As a warrior for godliness, Daniel gives us boldness to face the future and stay true to God. It is a sure thing: God's team will win. The battle may be fierce, but assurance of victory is ours according to the message of Daniel.

The Antichrist

The Antichrist lives up to his title: He is against Christ, and everything to do with Christ.

Toward the end of their kingdoms, when they have become morally rotten, an angry king shall rise to power with great shrewdness and intelligence. His power shall be mighty, but it will be satanic strength and not his own. Prospering wherever he turns, he will destroy all who oppose him, though their armies be mighty, and he will devastate God's people.

He will be a master of deception, defeating many by catching them off guard as they bask in false security. Without warning he will destroy them. So great will he fancy himself to be that he will even take on the Prince of Princes in battle; but in so doing he will seal his own doom, for he shall be broken by the hand of God, though no human means could overpower him. (Daniel 8:23–25, TLB)

While his power won't last forever, he will have global influence. People used to laugh at the Bible for making bold statements and saying someone would be known all over the earth. Then television arrived in the late 1940s. With advancing technology, one person can address the entire world with the press of a button. This Antichrist will have that ability. Notice how one author describes this world leader:

He will have the oratorical skill of a John Kennedy, the inspirational power of a Winston Churchill, the determination of a Joseph Stalin, the vision of a Karl Marx, the respectability of a

Ghandi, the military prowess of a Douglas Mac-Arthur, the charm of a Will Rogers, and the genius of a King Solomon. In addition, he will be empowered by Satan, and his incredible capabilities will be used against God's people.[1]

Daniel gives us another window to peer in as we look into the future of the Antichrist.

The king will do exactly as he pleases, claiming to be greater than every god there is, even blaspheming the God of gods, and prospering—until his time is up. For God's plans are unshakable. He will have no regard for the gods of his fathers, nor for the god beloved of women, nor any other god, for he will boast that he is greater than them all. Instead of these he will worship the Fortress god—a god his fathers never knew—and lavish on him costly gifts! Claiming his help he will have great success against the strongest fortresses. He will honor those who submit to him, appointing them to positions of authority and dividing the land to them as their reward.

Then at the time of the end, the king of the south will attack him again, and the northern king will react with the strength and fury of a whirlwind; his vast army and navy will rush out to bury him with their might. He will invade various lands on the way, including Israel, the Pleasant Land, and overthrow the governments of many nations. Moab, Edom, and most of

Ammon will escape, but Egypt and many other lands will be occupied. He will capture all the treasures of Egypt, and the Libyans and Ethiopians shall be his servants.

But then news from the east and north will alarm him and he will return in great anger to destroy as he goes. He will halt between Jerusalem and the sea, and there pitch his royal tents, but while he is there his time will suddenly run out and there will be no one to help him. (11:36–45, TLB)

His power will be seemingly unlimited, recognized and known everywhere. Yet, his days are numbered. He will be stopped—dead.

Those in Christ

Daniel also shows us several windows to peer through for those in Christ. The hardships appear insurmountable, but they won't last forever.

For I had seen this horn warring against God's people and winning, until the Ancient of Days came and opened his court and vindicated his people, giving them worldwide powers of government. . . .

He will defy the Most High God, and wear down the saints with persecution, and try to change all laws, morals, and customs. God's people will be helpless in his hands for three and a half years. (7:21–22, 25, TLB)

131

Because the Antichrist is against anything or anyone who stands for godliness, he will inflict intense brutality on those in Christ. We find this hope for believers, however.

> "But the saints of the Most High will receive the kingdom and will possess it forever—yes, for ever and ever."
> . . . until the Ancient of Days came and pronounced judgment in favor of the saints of the Most High, and the time came when they possessed the kingdom. (7:18, 22)

> At that time Michael, the great prince who protects your people, will arise. There will be a time of distress such as has not happened from the beginning of nations until then. But at that time your people—everyone whose name is found written in the book—will be delivered. Multitudes who sleep in the dust of the earth will awake: some to everlasting life, others to shame and everlasting contempt. Those who are wise will shine like the brightness of the heavens, and those who lead many to righteousness, like the stars for ever and ever. But you, Daniel, close up and seal the words of the scroll until the time of the end. Many will go here and there to increase knowledge. (12:1–4)

Because Christ has already won the battle over evil, and because we are in Christ, we win. Daniel's prediction is accurate, matching other sections of the

Bible. Therefore, we are not hopeless. Those who live for God as Daniel did will not have any regrets.

Christ Himself

As Daniel has spoken about the Antichrist and those in Christ, he also affirms what will happen regarding Christ.

As I looked,

thrones were set in place,
   and the Ancient of Days took his seat.
His clothing was as white as snow;
   the hair of his head was white like wool.
His throne was flaming with fire,
   and its wheels were all ablaze.
A river of fire was flowing,
   coming out from before him.
Thousands upon thousands attended him;
   ten thousand times ten thousand stood before
      him.
The court was seated,
   and the books were opened. (7:9–10)

In my vision at night I looked, and there before me was one like a son of man, coming with the clouds of heaven. He approached the Ancient of Days and was led into his presence. He was given authority, glory and sovereign power; all peoples, nations and men of every language worshiped him. His dominion is an everlasting dominion that will not pass away, and his kingdom is one that will never be destroyed. (7:13–14)

But the court will sit for judgment, and his dominion will be taken away, annihilated and destroyed forever. Then the sovereignty, the dominion, and the greatness of all the kingdoms under the whole heaven will be given to the people of the saints of the Highest One; His kingdom will be an everlasting kingdom, and all the dominions will serve and obey Him. (7:26–27, NASB)

As Daniel has recorded, God's people will be the ones who win as the Antichrist is forever defeated and removed. That is why modeling our life after Daniel will ultimately be worthwhile. Living like he did puts us on the team that wins the trophy.

Take the challenge to live like Daniel did. Serve God with all your life with no regrets. Let his life, a picture of a hero being built brick upon brick, be an example to you. Let the future Daniel tells about, and the confidence you have in Christ, be a reinforcement rod, stabilizing the very foundation of your being. One thing is for sure: those who serve the Lord will win. That's a promise.

Putting It into My Life

1. Daniel's life has been seen in many ways as we have peered through the various windows of this study. What has been something that has impacted you? How could it impact you within the

next six months? One year from now?

2. The Antichrist, those in Christ, and Christ Himself have been portrayed in this chapter. What new things did you learn? What confidences are now yours? In your opinion, is living life as Daniel did worthwhile? Why or why not?

3. The Antichrist and the end times are a great study. Here are some other references from the Bible that you may want to use in future studies:

Daniel 7:8; Revelation 6:1–2
Isaiah 28:15,18; Daniel 9:27
Revelation 13:1; 12:14
Revelation 17:11–14, 17; 18:2, 10, 16
2 Thessalonians 2:4; Matthew 24:15
Revelation 14:1–5; 17:16–17
Revelation 17:14; 19:19–20; 20:10

11

You—A Hero to Others

―――――

The study of Daniel has been fantastic. His story of a servant found faithful moves from chains to a champion, from abuse to awesome role model. His dedication is like a 1,000-watt light bulb turned on inside a dark, damp cave. He dispelled darkness and brought hope! Exercising faith in the God he worshiped, he set an undeniable example. No one can help being awe-struck by his relationship with the Lord. No matter what he faced—an unknown language and culture, a death sentence by an enraged king, friends being thrown into a stove like firewood, liars trying to trap him, invasions by other countries, and even a lions' den—Daniel is a cut above the rest. His consistency paid off. He is a role model, a warrior, a leader, a challenger and a hero all packed into one wallop! No one yawns studying the life of Daniel.

Needed — A Daniel for Today

In Chapter 1, I mentioned some heart-wrenching statistics that Dawson McAlister shared at a recent conference I attended. At that same meeting, he also gave the following information:

- 25% of American teens never open a Bible.
- 18 million single-parent homes exist in America.
- 1 in 3 girls and 1 in 6 guys are forced into a sexual encounter with an adult.
- 1 in 4 people killed in automobile accidents in America are because of a drunk teenager driving.
- 70% are susceptible to drugs.
- By 19 years of age, 80% of guys and girls aren't virgins.
- 85% of American teens have seen pornography by age 13.
- 1 of 4 guys at UCLA would rape a girl if they could get away with it.
- Depression is the #2 problem on Jr. and Sr. High Campuses (The #1 problem is the common cold).
- 1 in 6 attempt suicide in high school years.

Every day in America:
- 3,000 teens become pregnant.
- 372 babies are miscarried.
- 1,106 abortions are performed.
- 1,295 give birth.
- 10 children are killed by guns.
- 30 are wounded by guns.

- 5,500 attempt suicide.
- 135,000 take guns to school.
- 7,742 become sexually active.
- 623 get syphilis.
- 1 in 3,000 teens have AIDS.
- 211 are arrested for drug abuse.
- 437 are arrested for driving while under the influence of drugs or alcohol.
- 1,512 drop out of school.
- 1,849 are abused.
- 3,288 run away.
- 1,629 are put in adult jails.
- 2,556 babies are born out of wedlock.
- almost 3,000 see parents divorce.[1]

That is why we need heroes, "Daniels" today. People are crying, hurting, aching and calling. Teens today are searching for someone, somewhere to throw them a lifeline to rescue them from being sucked into a society that offers no hope.

It doesn't take a sociologist to figure out that our culture is on a downward spiral morally, spiritually, and emotionally. For example, your parents may have gotten into trouble at school for offenses that would likely be ignored today. Just look at this comparison of the top offenses in 1940 and 1980:

1940	*1980*
1) Talking	1) Rape
2) Chewing gum	2) Robbery
3) Running in the halls	3) Assault

4) Wearing improper clothing
5) Making noise
6) Not putting paper in wastebaskets
7) Getting out of turn in line

4) Personal theft

5) Burglary
6) Drug abuse

7) Arson

8) Bombings
9) Alcohol abuse
10) Carrying of weapons
11) Absenteeism
12) Vandalism
13) Murder
14) Extortion
15) Gang warfare
16) Pregnancies
17) Abortions
18) Suicide
19) Venereal disease
20) Lying and cheating[2]

Amazing! Do you see why the principles of Daniel's life need to be transferred to us today? Now is the time to take the challenge, to commit your total life to God's way, and ask Him to empower you for an impact in our world.

Be on the move for God. It takes vision to rescue people from darkness. Without hearing the cries and loneliness of others, there will be no difference made.

Once a girl named Annie heard the cries of

people. She herself had been rescued from personal pain and loneliness. She made the choice to take the risk to help. The world hasn't been the same since.

Annie was the oldest of three children. Her family had buried two other infants due to illness. By age nine, Anne had seen her mom die of tuberculosis, and her younger sister adopted by another family. Her younger brother was stricken with tuberculosis. Growing up, Annie had severe eye trouble, and was nearly blind due to infection and scarring of the eyeball. As though the death of her mother and siblings and her sister being adopted away from the family wasn't enough, her father also abandoned her and her brother Jimmy, age six. She never received a birthday present or Christmas present as a child. She had trouble finding a school she could attend, due to her poor family background and her weak eyes.

As abandoned children, Jimmy and Annie were taken in by family members, an arrangement which proved hopeless, due to Annie's violent temper. They ended up as wards of the state; the only facility available was a mental institution.

Annie and Jimmy were to live among the elderly, mentally deranged, and socially outcast for one year. When Annie was ten, Jimmy, the only hope and stability left in her life, died. Tuberculosis had claimed another victim in Annie's life. And despite six operations, she continued to lose her sight. All seemed hopeless.

Annie was determined not to quit. She approached a visitor at the institute for help, and soon was given a chance to attend Perkins Institute for the Blind in South Boston. Though she had never attended school, and at the age of 14 could not even spell her name, she was determined to make a difference.

At 16, after several operations, Annie's eyesight was restored. Soon she was advancing rapidly, and knew that she could help others. She worked hard in school and graduated valedictorian, the top of her class! She continued helping the blind, wanting to make an impact in her world. That opportunity came at age 20, when Annie received a letter from a couple in Alabama, asking her to come help their six-year-old daughter, who was blind and deaf. The girl's name was Helen Keller.

Annie took the challenge and changed the world of Helen Keller and the world of the blind and deaf. It wasn't without a cost, however. Listen to an encounter at the breakfast table:

> Their longest and most violent battle occurred one morning at the breakfast table. No one had ever tried to teach Helen to sit at the table and eat from her own plate with a spoon. Instead, she would run around the table, grabbing food off other people's plates and the dishes that were being passed while the family went on eating and talking as though nothing extraordinary was happening.
>
> That morning Helen started to grab some food off Annie's plate. Annie pushed her greasy hands away. Helen tried it again, and Annie slapped

141

her. Whereupon Helen threw herself on the floor, kicking and screaming. Annie lifted her up, set her down hard on the chair, forced a spoon into her hand and started to help her scoop up some food on it.

Helen threw the spoon on the floor. Annie dragged her down off the chair, made her pick up the spoon, set her back on the chair and started over again. But Helen hurled the spoon to the floor and threw herself on top of it.

At this point Captain and Mrs. Keller, who had been watching in horrified silence, got up and left the room, breakfast unfinished. Annie followed them up to the door, locked it behind them, returned to the table and went on eating her breakfast, although it nearly choked her.

Helen jumped up and tried to pull Annie's chair out from under her. When that didn't work, she pinched Annie, and Annie slapped her. That was repeated several times.

Finally, after another fit of kicking and screaming, Helen started to feel her way around the table. When she discovered that her parents' places were empty, she came back to Annie. She seemed puzzled and placed her hand on Annie's wrist. Raising her fork to her mouth, Annie indicated that she was eating. Helen hesitated for a moment, then climbed up on her chair and docilely permitted Annie to help her eat her breakfast with a spoon. Apparently, hunger had won out.[3]

Because of Annie's desire to impact her world, Helen Keller became the first blind and deaf person to learn to read and write, talk, and become educated. She graduated summa cum laude, second in her class, at Radcliffe College, an all-women's college associated with Harvard University. She also authored several books, was a speaker in every major city in America and much of Canada, and was the spokesperson for many organizations for the handicapped. She was even introduced to President Cleveland, and was invited to his second inauguration.

How did a blind and deaf girl get from the darkness of her world to the enlightenment of an education? What lifted her off the floor of the kitchen to the floor of many concert halls of our land? Who was responsible for her transition from not being able to speak to being able to communicate with the President of the United States? The answer is clear: Helen Keller was changed because a teenager had a vision. Annie Sullivan dared to take the challenge. In the process, she changed the world and its thinking toward the handicapped.

Our world is full of handicapped people. It is not just the blind, deaf, lame, and mentally ill who are impaired. People with normal capacities to walk, talk, see, hear, think and function in society also ache deeply. They cry out for someone to help and heal their hurts, lifting them from their despair. The abuse, sin, poor moral choices, broken homes and wounded spirits nearly suffocate them daily.

Perhaps you are thinking, "I'd like to do that, but I

don't have the right background," or, "I've never done anything like that before" or, "When I get my own life all together, I'll consider it." What if Annie Sullivan had waited? Suppose her thinking would have been: "When I get all healed up from my mother's death when I was nine, my family rejecting me, my brother's death and my being reared in a mental institution, then I will take a challenge." Imagine how different things would have been if she had said: "When my eyes are healed, I will do something." Had she responded that way, our world would be no different. You see, Annie never was completely released from the pain of her past, and shortly before she died, her eyes were so bad that she had to hold a book to her nose to be able to read it. Annie became a hero, taking the challenge, despite the high risks. Was it worth it? Listen to Helen's recollection of the first day her world was introduced to Annie Sullivan:

Have you ever been at sea in a dense fog, when it seemed as if a tangible white darkness shut you in, and the great ship tense and anxious, groped her way toward the shore with plummet and sounding-line, and you waited with beating heart for something to happen? I was like that ship before my education began, only without a compass or sounding-line, and had no way of knowing how near the harbor was. "Light! give me light!" was the wordless cry of my soul, and the light of love shone on me in that very hour.
I felt approaching footsteps. I stretched out my

hand as I supposed it was my mother. Some one took it, and I was caught up and held close in the arms of her who had come to reveal all things to me, and, more than all things else, to love me.[4]

Those who have been rescued are indebted, grateful, and forever changed because of the compassion of another. Just listen to the difference made in Helen Keller's life from that day Annie Sullivan entered the darkness and liberated her:

We walked down the path to the well-house, attracted by the fragrance of the honeysuckle with which it was covered. Someone was drawing water and my teacher placed my hand under the spout. As the cool stream gushed over one hand she spelled into the other the word "water", first slowly, then rapidly. I stood still, my whole attention fixed upon the motions of her fingers. Suddenly I felt a misty consciousness as of something forgotten—a thrill of returning thought; and somehow the mystery of language was revealed to me. I knew then that "w-a-t-e-r" meant the wonderful cool something that was flowing over my hand. That living word awakened my soul, gave it light, hope, joy, set it free! There were barriers still, it is true, but barriers that in time could be swept away. . . . I learned a great many new words that day. I do not remember what they all were; but I do know that "mother", "father", "sister", "teacher" were among them—words that were to make the world blossom for me, "like Aaron's rod, with flowers." It would have been difficult to find a happier child than I was as I lay in my crib at the close of that eventful day and lived over the joys today had brought me, and for the first time longed for a new day to come.[5]

You — in the Hall of Heroes

How about you? Will you shake off the chains of yesterday's pain, and move out for God? Will you see and hear the despair of others and take the challenge to reshape their world? Will you become a hero to the multi-impaired society we live in? If you will, you'll be in good company:

> I'm convinced that unswerving commitment to a person, a cause, or an idea is the single quality that gives life its vitality. Think how Thomas Edison felt when he dreamed of a lamp that could burn invisible energy. He could have quit, and no one would have blamed him. After all, he had more than ten thousand failures in that one project alone. Chances are you and I haven't had that many failures during all our lifetimes combined.
>
> The Wright brothers wanted to do more than repair bikes in their Dayton, Ohio, bicycle shop, so they dreamed of a machine that could ride the sky. Some laughed at them; others said it was not God's will for men to fly. But Orville and Wilbur determined to follow their dream. On

December 17, 1903, near Kitty Hawk, North Carolina, history was made as the first power-driven airplane roared into the sky.

Daniel Webster could not make a speech until after years of disciplined effort but became one of America's greatest orators. George Washington lost more battles than he won but triumphed in the end. Winners never quit, and quitters never win. A cliche, but still true. If you don't believe it, consider these examples.

John Bunyan wrote *Pilgrim's Progress* while languishing in Bedford Prison in England, locked up for his vocal views on religion . . .

Charles Dickens began his illustrious career with the unimpressive job of pasting labels on blacking pots. The tragedy of his first love shot through to the depths of his soul, touching off a genius of creativity that made him one of the greatest authors of all time.

Robert Burns was an illiterate country boy; O. Henry, a criminal and an outcast; Beethoven, deaf; Milton, blind. But once they mastered their own weaknesses and committed themselves to service, they strengthened the soul of all humanity.

Are you prepared to master your own weakness? The three greatest words in the English language for gaining fulfillment are DO IT NOW. Work on your commitments prayerfully. Don't wait. DO IT NOW.[6]

It's true: you can be a hero to others, although it

won't be pain-free. Being in the "Hall of Heroes" doesn't come without paying the price of consistency, dedication, and even a broken heart at times. But just as Daniel dared to make a difference, so you have to make a choice too.

Enlist in the ranks of the "risk-takers." Take the leadership, and see the world as it is: hopeless, weary, wounded, and needing a hero. Daniel did and never regretted it. What a way to live!

The world is waiting for someone with guts and answers. The Lord will supply both to those who dare to make a difference.

Go for it!

12

Jesus—Hero of Heroes

━━━━

I n **Chapter 1 we said every** hero has a hero. We all need what heroes give—courage, role models, hope, ideas, and patterns worth following. The call is to take the challenge and make a difference. I hope you will become a hero because you see what God could do through the life of one teenager, Daniel. We need world-changers, and teens with a vision to call people back to the truths of God. That won't happen overnight, but with consistency and time, it will take place.

For that vision to remain fresh, we need someone to pattern our lives after. Even heroes need heroes. And the greatest hero of all time was Jesus. He will always shine as the greatest example, role model and hero the world has ever encountered. Look what the Bible says about Him.

He was the creator of all:

> Through him all things were made; without him nothing was made that has been made. (John 1:3)

> He is the image of the invisible God, the firstborn over all creation. For by him all things were created: things in heaven and on earth, visible and invisible, whether thrones or powers or rulers or authorities; all things were created by him and for him. He is before all things, and in him all things hold together. (Colossians 1:15–17)

> You are worthy, our Lord and God,
>   to receive glory and honor and power,
> for you created all things,
>   and by your will they were created
>   and have their being. (Revelation 4:11)

This same God-man also came to earth to live among people, interacting with them in their hurts, illnesses, hopelessness and weariness, offering them hope.

> Blessed are the poor in spirit,
>   for theirs is the kingdom of heaven.
> Blessed are those who mourn,
>   for they will be comforted.
> Blessed are the meek,
>   for they will inherit the earth.

Blessed are those who hunger and thirst for
    righteousness,
  for they will be filled. (Matthew 5:3–6)

When he came down from the mountainside,
large crowds followed him. A man with leprosy
came and knelt before him and said, "Lord, if
you are willing, you can make me clean."

Jesus reached out his hand and touched the
man. "I am willing," he said. "Be clean!" Immediately he was cured of his leprosy. (8:1–3)

While he was saying this, a ruler came and
knelt before him and said, "My daughter has just
died. But come and put your hand on her, and
she will live." Jesus got up and went with him,
and so did his disciples.

Just then a women who had been subject to
bleeding for twelve years came up behind him
and touched the edge of his cloak. She said to
herself, "If I only touch his cloak, I will be
healed."

Jesus turned and saw her. "Take heart,
daughter," he said, "your faith has healed you."
And the woman was healed from that moment.

When Jesus entered the ruler's house and saw
the flute players and the noisy crowd, he said,
"Go away. The girl is not dead but asleep." But
they laughed at him. After the crowd had been
put outside, he went in and took the girl by the
hand, and she got up. News of this spread
through all that region. (9:18–26)

Though He lived with sinful people and those who had given in to temptation, and though He was tempted Himself, He never sinned.

> At once the Spirit sent him out into the desert, and he was in the desert forty days, being tempted by Satan. He was with the wild animals, and angels attended him. (Mark 1:12–13)

> Because he himself suffered when he was tempted, he is able to help those who are being tempted. (Hebrews 2:18)

> Therefore, since we have a great high priest who has gone through the heavens, Jesus the Son of God, let us hold firmly to the faith we profess. For we do not have a high priest who is unable to sympathize with our weaknesses, but we have one who has been tempted in every way, just as we are—yet was without sin. Let us then approach the throne of grace with confidence, so that we may receive mercy and find grace to help us in our time of need. (4:14–16)

Not only did He come to our earth and live with sinful people and was tempted like we are, but He remained pure and gave His sinlessness for our sin.

> When they came to the place called the Skull, there they crucified him, along with the criminals—one on his right, the other on his left. Jesus said, "Father, forgive them, for they do not

know what they are doing." And they divided up his clothes by casting lots. (Luke 23:33–34)

God made him who had no sin to be sin for us, so that in him we might become the righteousness of God. (2 Corinthians 5:21)

After His death, He also came back to life, defeating man's arch-enemies, the devil and death.

The God of peace will soon crush Satan under your feet. (Romans 16:20)

These are some of the reasons Jesus is the Hero of heroes. He left heaven, came to earth, lived a sinless life, gave it up for us, and rose from the dead.

Daniel saw the power and truth of Jesus when he interpreted the first dream for King Nebuchadnezzar. Included in the dream was an awesome, dazzling statue. The head was of gold, its arms and chest were silver, the belly and thighs were made of bronze, and the legs of iron, and the feet had both iron and clay. However, Nebuchadnezzar saw a rock hit this statue, smashing it to pieces. This deeply troubled the king, who then sought for an interpretation. When no one could give the meaning, he called for everyone's death, including Daniel's. At this point, Daniel asked for a chance to tell and interpret the dream, and permission was granted. Daniel then explained the dream as the Lord had told him what it meant, and who it was about.

This was the dream, and now we will interpret it to the king. You, O king, are the king of kings. The God of heaven has given you dominion and power and might and glory; in your hands he has placed mankind and the beasts of the field and the birds of the air. Wherever they live, he has made you ruler over them all. You are that head of gold.

After you, another kingdom will rise, inferior to yours. Next a third kingdom, one of bronze, will rule over the whole earth. Finally, there will be a fourth kingdom, strong as iron—for iron breaks and smashes everything—and as iron breaks things to pieces, so it will crush and break all the others. Just as you saw that the feet and toes were partly of baked clay and partly of iron, so this will be a divided kingdom; yet it will have some of the strength of iron in it, even as you saw iron mixed with clay. As the toes were partly iron and partly clay, so this kingdom will be partly strong and partly brittle. And just as you saw the iron mixed with baked clay, so the people will be a mixture and will not remain united, any more than iron mixes with clay.

In the time of those kings, the God of heaven will set up a kingdom that will never be destroyed, nor will it be left to another people. It will crush all those kingdoms and bring them to an end, but it will itself endure forever. This is the meaning of the vision of the rock cut out of a mountain, but not by human hands—a rock that broke the iron, the bronze, the clay, the silver and the gold to pieces.

The great God has shown the king what will take place in the future. The dream is true and the interpretation is trustworthy. (Daniel 2:36–45)

The kingdom of the Lord Jesus will be one that will reign forever. Evil will be destroyed. When Jesus comes to establish His kingdom, there will be no more crying, sorrow, sin, wickedness, slavery, abuse or molestation. All satanic powers will fizzle out like a wet firecracker. That is the reason Jesus is the Hero of heroes. The whole world will acknowledge this.

Therefore God exalted him to the highest place
and gave him the name that is above
every name,
that at the name of Jesus every knee should bow,
in heaven and on earth and under the earth,
and every tongue confess that Jesus Christ
is Lord,
to the glory of God the Father.
(Philippians 2:9–11)

In the last days

the mountain of the LORD's temple will be
established
as chief among the mountains;
it will be raised above the hills,
and all nations will stream to it.

Many peoples will come and say,

"Come, let us go up to the mountain of the
     LORD,
  to the house of the God of Jacob.
He will teach us his ways,
  so that we may walk in his paths."
The law will go out from Zion,
  the word of the LORD from Jerusalem.
He will judge between the nations
  and will settle disputes for many peoples.
They will beat their swords into plowshares
  and their spears into pruning hooks.
Nation will not take up sword against nation,
  nor will they train for war anymore.
    (Isaiah 2:2–4)

From you comes the theme of my praise in the
     great assembly;
  before those who fear you will I fulfill my
     vows.
The poor will eat and be satisfied;
  they who seek the LORD will praise him—
  may your hearts live forever!
All the ends of the earth
  will remember and turn to the LORD,
and all the families of the nations
  will bow down before him,
for dominion belongs to the LORD
  and he rules over the nations.
    (Psalm 22:25–28)

In Christ all mankind will be complete. He will be acknowledged as the King of kings, and Lord of lords, and will also reward those who have served as heroes in His name.

> Now there is in store for me the crown of righteousness, which the Lord, the righteous Judge, will award to me on that day—and not only to me, but also to all who have longed for his appearing. (2 Timothy 4:8)

> Do not be afraid of what you are about to suffer. I tell you, the devil will put some of you in prison to test you, and you will suffer persecution for ten days. Be faithful even to the point of death, and I will give you the crown of life. (Revelation 2:10)

What a day that will be. We will all worship, live and adore Christ forever. There will be no regrets that day for those who have been faithful. Daniel was a hero, and gave the credit to the Lord, so we will also. Just look at these promises:

> The twenty-four elders fall down before him who sits on the throne, and worship him who lives forever and ever. They lay their crowns before the throne and say:

> "You are worthy, our Lord and God,
>   to receive glory and honor and power,
>   for you created all things,

and by your will they were created
and have their being."
   (4:10–11)

Then I saw a new heaven and a new earth, for the first heaven and the first earth had passed away, and there was no longer any sea. I saw the Holy City, the new Jerusalem, coming down out of heaven from God, prepared as a bride beautifully dressed for her husband. And I heard a loud voice from the throne saying, "Now the dwelling of God is with men, and he will live with them. They will be his people; and God himself will be with them and be their God. He will wipe every tear from their eyes. There will be no more death or mourning or crying or pain, for the old order of things has passed away."

He who was seated on the throne said, "I am making everything new!" Then he said, "Write this down, for these words are trustworthy and true."

He said to me: "It is done. I am the Alpha and the Omega, the Beginning and the End. To him who is thirsty I will give to drink without cost from the spring of the water of life. He who overcomes will inherit all this, and I will be his God and he will be my son. (21:1–7)

Then the angel showed me the river of the water of life, as clear as crystal, flowing from the throne of God and of the Lamb down the middle of the great street of the city. On each side of the river stood the tree of life, bearing twelve crops of fruit, yielding its fruit every month. And the leaves of the tree are for healing of the nations. No longer will there be any curse. The throne of God and of the Lamb will be in the city, and his servants will serve him. They will see his face, and his name will be on their foreheads. There will be no more night. They will not need the light of a lamp or of the sun, for the Lord God will give them light. And they will reign for ever and ever. (22:1–5)

What hope! What majesty! And it will all revolve around one person—Jesus Christ, the Hero of heroes. Everything else will crumble, crash and end up as a huge pile of ashes.

My final challenge to you who read this book about Daniel is that you choose to spend your life becoming a hero like Daniel. When Jesus comes again, you won't be ashamed.

Go for it! On that day when we see Him, the Hero of heroes, it will be worth it all!

Notes

Chapter 1

1. Anthony Campolo. *Who Switched The Price Tags?* (Dallas, TX: Word Books, 1986), pp. 46–47.
2. Fred Hartley. *What's Right, What's Wrong in an Upside Down World.* (Atlanta, GA: Oliver Nelson Books, 1988), pp. 9–10.
3. Dawson McAlister, speaking at the Annual Council of The Christian and Missionary Alliance, Washington D.C., May 26, 1990.
4. "This Year's Role Model." *Newsweek* (special edition), Summer/Fall 1990, pp. 45–47.

Chapter 2

1. *Insights Magazine.* Insight For Living, Charles Swindoll, senior editor, Spring 1984.

Chapter 3

1. Charles Swindoll. *You and Your Problems.* (Fullerton, CA: Insight For Living, 1989), p. 50.
2. Charles Swindoll. *Encourage Me: Caring Words for Heavy Hearts.* (Portland, OR: Multnomah Press, 1982), p. 79.
3. "Mike Warnke—Alive." cassette tape (Dallas, TX:

Word Books, 1976).

Chapter 4

1. Sally Magnusson. *The Flying Scotsman.* (New York: Quartet Books, 1981), p. 165.
2. Tony Campolo. *You Can Make a Difference.* (Dallas, TX: Word Books, 1984), pp. 24–25.
3. Richard Harvey. *70 Years of Miracles.* (Beaverlodge, AB: Horizon House, 1977), pp. 64–66.
4. Fred Hartley. *100%.* (Old Tappan, NJ: Fleming H. Revell, 1983), p. 152.
5. Jack W. Hayford. *Rebuilding the Real You.* (Ventura, CA: Regal Books, 1986), pp. 70–71.

Chapter 5

1. Les Morgan. *Pulling Weeds.* (Camp Hill, PA: Christian Publications, 1989), pp.20–21.
2. Hartley. *100%.* pp. 76–77.

Chapter 6

1. Les Morgan. *Here's A Hero: Joseph.* (Camp Hill, PA: Christian Publications, 1990), pp. 9–10.
2. Billy Graham Evangelistic Association newsletter, July 1989.
3. Gordon MacDonald. *Restoring Your Spiritual Passion.* (Atlanta, GA: Oliver Nelson, 1986), pp. 13–14.

Chapter 7

1. James Dobson. *Straight Talk to Men and Their Wives.* (Dallas, TX: Word Books, 1980), pp. 58–60.

Chapter 8

1. Ted W. Engstrom. *The Pursuit of Excellence.* (Grand Rapids, MI: Zondervan, 1982), pp. 81–82.
2. Morgan. *Here's A Hero: Joseph.* p. 69.
3. Art Linkletter. *Principles for Successful Living* (cassette recording). (Chicago: Nightingale-Conant Corp., 1983).
4. Emily Morison Beck (ed.). *John Barlett's Familiar Quotations* 15th and 125th Anniversary eds. (Boston: Little Brown and Company, 1855, 1980), p. 79.

Chapter 9

1. Insight For Living Newsletter, April 1990. (Fullerton, CA: Insight for Living).
2. Charles R. Swindoll. *Esther, A Woman For Such a Time As This.* (Fullerton, CA: Insight for Living, 1991), p. 40.
3. Richard J. Foster. *Celebration of Discipline.* (San Francisco, CA: Harper & Row, 1978), p. 1.
4. Philip P. Bliss. "Dare to Be a Daniel." *Hymns of the Christian Life.* (Camp Hill, PA: Christan Publications, 1962).

Chapter 10

1. Charles R. Swindoll. *Daniel, God's Pattern For The Future.* (Fullerton, CA: Insight For Living, 1986), p. 70.

Chapter 11

1. Dawson McAlister, speaking at Annual Council of The Christian and Missionary Alliance, Washington

D.C., May 26, 1990.

2. Dan Adams. *The Child Influence: Restoring the Lost Art of Parenting.* (Cuyahoga Falls, OH: Home Team Press, 1990), p. 171. (Quoted from private research conducted by Cullen Davis, P.O. Box 1224, Ft. Worth TX).

3. Lorena A. Hickok. *A Touch of Magic.* (New York: Dodd, Mead and Company, 1963), p. 58–59.

4. Helen Keller, as quoted in *Turning Point,* ed. Phillip Dunaway and George de Kay. (New York: Random House, 1958), pp. 105-106.

5. Keller, ibid., pp. 106–107.

6. Ted W. Engstrom with Robert C. Larson. *A Time for Commitment.* (Grand Rapids, MI: Zondervan, 1987), pp. 29–30.

Christian Publications acknowledges the kindness of the following publishers for allowing the use of extended quotes from their material:

Fleming H. Revell Company for footnote 2 in Chapter 5 which was taken from the book *100%* by Fred Hartley. Copyright © 1983 by Fred Hartley. Used by permission of Fleming H. Revell Company.

Zondervan Publishing House for footnote 1 in Chapter 8 which was taken from the book *The Pursuit of Excellence* by Ted W. Engstrom. Copyright © 1982 by Zondervan Publishing House. Used by permission of Zondervan Publishing House.

Zondervan Publishing House for footnote 6 in Chapter 11 which was taken from the book *A Time for Commitment* by Ted W. Engstrom with Robert C. Larson. Copyright © 1987 by Ted W. Engstrom. Used by permission of Zondervan Publishing House.